NATURE AT HEART

—

FOR A BETTER WORLD

TRANSLATED FROM THE FRENCH BY
MARK AND JAMES HARVEY

GÉRARD BERTRAND

NATURE AT HEART

—

FOR A BETTER WORLD

TRANSLATED FROM THE FRENCH BY
MARK AND JAMES HARVEY

ACC ART BOOKS

THANK YOU is how sharing begins, a mark of respect, the impulse of the heart

that connects people, and gratitude towards our planet, which hosts us with such generosity.

Thank you is also learning lessons without needing to give any, and having the humility

to understand that we are here because nature has created us.

Thank you for the water we drink, the air we breathe, the sun which warms us and

the biodiversity that feeds all living beings.

Thank you to all those who are willing to change yet do not want to change everything.

To my family, my fellow travelers along the way, and to all human beings who have

nature at heart.

PREFACE

The present-day world is fascinating and inspiring, but also alarming and worrying.

Both power and fragility have reached a peak and the flow of digital information imposes its speed upon our lives.

The Internet has eradicated distance and is organizing a new society which is overturning our age-old art of living.

The Covid-19 crisis has engendered a devastating pandemic on a global scale but, paradoxically, has given some heaven-sent breathing space to those whose lives were being driven at a frantic pace. The health crisis quickly provoked economic and financial problems of unparalleled magnitude.

My purpose is to muster all the aspects of my personal and professional experience to offer an honest portrayal of today's world as seen through the lens of my convictions and life path.

Over the past forty years, I have gained much from the competitive spirit of rugby-playing at a high level, and exploring the values of sharing and pushing one's limits. I was introduced to wine-growing by my parents, and inspired by the vision that my father, Georges, nurtured for his land in the Languedoc. His insistence on putting into practice his flashes of inspiration around the blending of wines has guided me towards excellence and careful attention to innumerable details.

Pivotal encounters during this period have provided fertile soil for personal development. I have also been able, by regarding challenges as blessings that would allow me to grow and move forward, to sense the sometimes hidden meaning of things.

My awareness of nature was awakened, and my ardor in favor of biodiversity ignited, after I experienced the beneficial effects of homeopathy on my health, and subsequently read Rudolf Steiner's courses for farmers.

Baring my soul in this way has demanded courage, thoroughness, and honesty, all in the service of a cause and impetus that are greater than myself.

My commitment to values such as fellowship, loving one's neighbor, loving-kindness, respect for nature, but also an innate need to create, innovate and explore new avenues, stimulates my mind and strengthens my determination.

This book, then, puts forward an unorthodox framework of thought, generous and philanthropic, based on five pillars: an expansion of consciousness, transcendence, the liberation of feelings, care for the Earth and the challenges and issues comprised in a new humanism. The third millennium which has just begun has opened up a space of infinite potential and demands a disciplined approach and profound, unsettling reflection for a human race in quest of new points of reference.

Men and women today must face unprecedented challenges in order to make the transition to an innovative era which will inevitably differ from the 20th century. Making the right decisions will require individual and political courage and heartfelt fervor driving generosity and altruism. Public organizations, at global, continental, national, regional and local levels will need sincere, militant commitment to work out future benefits and priorities. Nothing will be possible or lasting without a worldwide awakening of the consciousness of humankind.

Urgency is not a reliable or comforting guide. Modern man has gained sufficient experience and has lived through more than enough crises and disasters to avoid rushing blindly into social models devoid of compassion and social connection. Spirituality, harmony with nature, stability on the personal and social levels will pave the way for a brighter future for all. Our collective and individual fears and anxiety, intensified by this world crisis, must on no account sacrifice our vital force on the altar of conformism and standardization. Conquering fear demands determination that nurtures confidence, with the liberation of feelings and ideas.

Our commitment to organic and biodynamic agriculture has enabled us to conduct large-scale experiments on the relevance of this model, especially in relation to wine-growing.

Taking care of the Earth has become a priority. This will require bold decisions and an innovative approach to the planet. The climate, the oceans, the forests, but also the pollinators, the soils and living species are all suffering from human activity. Biodiversity is in steep decline and deregulation has become a threat to life on Earth regarded with almost universal indifference. Respecting ecology is an act of civic duty that requires open-mindedness imbued with clarity and transnational alliances at the service of the biosphere, because pollution and global warming know no frontiers.

Our commitment to organic and biodynamic agriculture has enabled us to conduct large-scale experiments on the relevance of this model, especially in relation to wine-growing. A living soil strengthens the plants growing in it and helps them to capture the life forces emanating from the sun and the planets.

Research and science have invented new avenues and offered a way of escape from obscurantism while developing a technology opening the way to a transhumanism that advocates the use of technical aids to enhance the physical and mental capacities of humankind.

Here the human race is exhibiting its arrogance and complacency. If we measured the length of existence of the human race on a scale where one year represents that of the Earth, we would be surprised to learn that we have only been around for 28 seconds.

No matter whether we are religious or agnostic, either the hand of God or natural evolution is responsible for our presence here and gives us the power to control this planet. Until the Industrial Revolution in the middle of the 18th century, the human race was sedentary and had close ties to nature. There was gradual evolution for two hundred thousand years, followed by a frenzy of creativity in progress today. We are living in a very exciting period of history, in which everyone has the opportunity to take control of their life and invent their own future, except in countries where a dictatorship of ideas or power holds this energy in check. We live in a hyperconnected world in which the conditions, duration and quality of life have been much improved. In the so-called civilized countries, the art of living and hedonism, but also navel-gazing and egoism have become the points of reference of this new consumer society.

Our ecosystem is overheating; whistle-blowers of every hue demand our attention and beg us to respect Pachamama, the Earth-Mother revered by Andean peoples.

The human race, as if struck blind, is rushing headlong towards a catastrophe augured by changes to the climate, bush fires, galloping population growth, the concentration of men and women in dehumanized megalopolitan conurbations. From Australopithecus more than four million years ago, through *Homo habilis, Homo erectus, Homo neanderthalensis* and *Homo sapiens,* the evolution of species has developed the human race, leading it to walk erect and increase its intellectual and cognitive powers.

Insidiously, intensive use of the mobile phone has tilted our posture by twenty degrees.

Artificial intelligence, digital communication and numerous other artifacts are the instruments of the present-day economy. They should be used for good purposes and not be allowed to trespass upon the hard-won individual liberties of our ancestors, because there can be no love without freedom.

Progress is essential to the human condition to improve our lives but, taking a broader view, it must also take into account a respect for future generations in order to preserve the foundations of our lives and ensure the quality of our air, water, soils and the resources of our planet, which are not inexhaustible. Ultraliberalism, global competition and innovation stimulate the development of information and technologies. These three in alliance threaten the continuance of millions of jobs. "Big data" has become the "big deal" of the century.

There is purpose in growth, which gives everyone the chance to find fulfillment and bring their projects to completion, but it must also be useful, directed to the common good and respectful of the terrestrial and cosmic environment.

This is a priority, because there is no Plan B. We have to repair the damage inflicted on our Earth during the last fifty years and return to a baseline of harmony and sustainability: in short, a resilient society.

The environment could be protected by a process of ecological transition on a worldwide scale, setting and verifying standards in waste reduction, the energy mix and the control of global warming.

Human beings, individually and collectively, need to move forward from the paradigm of fear to that of love, empathy and tolerance. Religions must cease to be a source of conflict, since there is only one God, who bears different names, depending on our place of birth. Without tolerance, there is no religion. Let us seek what unites us, and not what divides us.

Each individual person is a sanctuary, our body is our temple and our vehicle. It is our duty to take care of it, listen to it and create the conditions for transcendence which will give us the courage to explore new horizons and go beyond the dogmas imposed by society, family, conventions and beliefs.

Becoming ourselves, giving birth to our inner self, understanding that there is that of God in every person, this is an exercise essential for fulfillment, of ourselves and others. It is a profession of faith and an encouragement which will show the way to those who believe.

We are limited and incarnate, but our spiritual power is limitless. Since Abraham, the father of the Jewish, Christian and Muslim religions, and subsequently Moses, Elijah, the Buddha, Alexander, Socrates, Caesar, Jesus, Mohammed and, more recently, Goethe, Rudolf Steiner, Mother Teresa and Nelson Mandela, prophets and exceptional individuals have each carried their epochs forward. They have asserted their beliefs and their clear-sighted vision and, in the case of some with a connection to God, have improved the human condition and set up precepts for living with far-reaching effects. Philosophies, religions, lessons in living and democracy have set the human soul free in trouble and suffering, but also in joy and delight.

We stand on the threshold of a new era, which will demand courage, solidarity and a disruptive vision.

A utopia; but utopia is a concept which links philosophy, humanism and spirituality in the service of an ideal social and political system, unrealistic to the skeptic but conceivable to those who dream of a better future.

PART I
AN AWAKENING OF CONSCIOUSNESS

·1·
SPIRITUALITY AND MATERIALISM

From the Industrial Revolution to the present day, the world has undergone greater changes than it had in all the centuries before.

All these periods, from the domination of Greek thought to Roman rule and, later, the Renaissance, laid the groundwork for the modern era. It is true that the Middle Ages dragged on in Western nations, with successive generations subjected to obscurantism, famine and alienation. The Renaissance released extraordinary creative energy and united politics and the economy. The geniuses of this period were the forerunners of modern times, in that they expanded our horizons and furthered changes in our condition as humans. Man has always pondered the meaning of life and the usefulness of his span of days between birth and death. Religious scriptures have imposed a rhythm upon life on earth. The present-day world rests upon the Jewish soul, Hellenic thought, Christian transcendence, Hindu and Buddhist nirvana, Muslim faith and Roman law.

The beginning of the 20th century was scarred by the wars from 1914 to 1918 and then 1939 to 1945, both with Germany as their epicenter. The first conflict having ended in her defeat, the resulting humiliation, combined with harsh living conditions, led to vengeful sentiments and fanatical nationalism. The second and even more murderous world war sealed a new alliance between Western forces and Russia, which laid the foundations for a new world and the United Nations – no subsequent major conflict has ever pitted the great nations of the world against each other. A measure of political stability ensued, made possible by the Yalta Conference and the Marshall Plan, which enabled economic development for countries open to international trade. The Eastern Bloc, however, continued to lag behind until perestroika, which was instituted by Mikhail Gorbachev and found the support of Pope John Paul II and the strength of his convictions.

For the past fifty years, we have enjoyed a golden era, characterized by continuously improved standards of living on our planet, except in large parts of Africa which still suffer from malnutrition, poverty and drinking water shortages. This part of the world and a few similar, more isolated cases, and certain countries in the grip of dictators such as North Korea aside, the liberalization of trade, movement of goods, services and food products, as well as the exponential growth of travel and tourism, have transformed the priorities of each one of us. In the past thirty years, we have consumed more energy and minerals than over the course of more than five millennia. We are living on credit and exhausting the resources of the earth, which cannot be replenished in such a short time.

We are living on credit and exhausting the resources of the earth, which cannot be replenished in such a short time.

This turbulent period has caused a momentous shift in behaviors and profound changes in the fabric of society. We have gone from perceiving the needs of all to focusing on the increased needs of the individual, and from a centuries-old structure to increased self-centeredness and individualism. The first two decades of the 21st century have served only to accelerate this process, weakening political systems up against economic giants attempting to control the world. These corporations have used the emergence of the Internet to weave a web which extends its tentacles across the world, creating new needs and services.

The time has come to reassess where we stand and set a new course for humanity. This will only be possible if our reasoning takes into account the multidimensional nature of human beings. The past decade has unchained creativity, research, and interaction in the service of better standards of living while also supporting the pursuit of pleasure and individualism in the wealthiest countries; however, exponential population growth has been the final whistle for playtime.

In the space of a hundred and fifty years, our planet has gone from being home to one and a half billion people to almost eight billion today. This has created substantial needs in energy, and a sizable challenge in waste management. As for the population growth forecasts for the next eighty years, they are inconceivable. How can we feed twelve billion human beings, whose life expectancy will no doubt increase? The two major challenges we face are global warming and the capacity of our planet to guarantee healthy and varied food for its population. All elements are interconnected: clear, mutually supportive answers will be needed, and lifestyle changes which will likely be painful if we do not act swiftly.

All of the above points to a preliminary question: is humanity both conscious of these issues and ready to change?

Nature is more powerful and more intelligent than we are: she is omniscient, self-sufficient and self-sustaining, as long as humans do not start aspiring to be masters of the game. Climate change is simply the consequence of the disruption of our natural ecosystems' rhythms. The modern world has lost the awareness of the intricate systems that created life on earth, from the first bacteria to human beings. Living standards are so much higher than fifty years ago that we take them for granted and live in denial of reality. Affordable electricity, ubiquitous air-conditioning, a continuous supply of goods and services and the flow of information have made abundance widespread and created a norm which, paradoxically, is extremely abnormal. As some experts say – not without a trace of humor – it is too late to be pessimistic. Only a rapid rise in awareness can reduce the excesses at the root of conflicts, wars and competition profitable only to the few and detrimental to the many.

For some, science represents the alpha and the omega of the survival of our species, and science alone will guarantee its progress by creating new resources and new means of communication. It has undeniably contributed to meeting the needs of an exponentially growing population, in terms of agricultural productivity and the establishment of transport networks both overland and by air. It has also made possible the regression, or even the eradication, of afflictions such as plague, cholera and tuberculosis. Furthermore, research on the atom, the relativity of time and quantum physics is opening up a new and fascinating field of exploration. And yet, the imbalance between Man and nature is increasingly worrying. Modern society, rushing headlong down a path based on the idea of never-ending progress, has created a monster whose guiding principle is growth. It is what safeguards the stability of the current materialistic model.

In the ancient civilizations of Egypt, Greece or Asia Minor, the connection between man and nature defined the pace of society's evolution. For centuries, mythology was the fabric of belief systems which helped to organize life on this earthly plane. The spiritual dimension was far more important than it is today. It was linked to the rhythm of the seasons: picking, farming, the making of the commodities necessary for community living. Human beings would implore the gods for their grace in meeting their precious needs, praying for rain, fertility, abundant harvests and divine protection. In spite of living conditions more challenging than ours, and shorter lives, anticipation of an afterlife was a part of their reality. A legacy of these highly spiritual civilizations remains in the form of the Egyptian pyramids, the Parthenon, Roman temples, and the surviving vestiges of Solomon's temple.

Without wishing to portray the past in an ideal light, the excessive selfishness in the world today is nevertheless a threat to the stability of a sustainable system. Nowadays, an insistence upon proof and the progress of science have resulted in the rise of skepticism and the questioning of human organizations, alongside reinforced individualism and a pseudo-freeing of consciences. The violence and injustices of the current system, the loss of biodiversity and the threats linked to global warming and the health crisis of 2020 have all required of us a change in pace, one which strikes a balance between material and spiritual needs.

André Malraux, in premonitory fashion, wrote that the 21st century would either be spiritual, or would not happen. A new era is beginning for humanity, which can support the transition from a hard, fierce and aggressive period to a world more humane, generous and conscious.

Our conscience is faced with an existential question of great relevance: that of the meaning of our incarnation in this time-bound world and of the consequences of our actions. We need to unearth once again our spiritual urges and the trinity of mind, body and spirit. Modern science and the quantum mindset can be put to work in the service of a transcendent evolution of humankind, in symbiosis with the forces of the universe.

Time is a recent human invention based upon the cycles of astronomical bodies. According to Steiner, a human being functions according to cycles: seven years for a set of teeth, seven more for puberty and, seven years later, at the age of twenty-one, he is considered complete and having reached adulthood. A plant is renewed and regenerated over a one-year cycle. The time scale for the formation of an astronomical object, such as a planet, and its integration into a solar system, is so far removed from our earthly time as to be unfathomable.

Ancient so-called calendar civilizations, such as the Mayans or the Chaldeans, pondered the influence of the planets and their role in the cosmos. Our materialistic age has a tendency to disconnect people from their inner, most intimate selves, because they are too busy with their work and their numerous distractions. In spite of the urgency of a spiritual awakening and the search for meaning, we seem to have ceased to pay attention to the great cosmic clock.

The mobile phone has become the compass of the new generation. Days have become too short to fulfill our needs. After an average of eight hours' sleep, there are sixteen useful hours left, a good proportion of which are spent connected to digital interfaces for the majority of those whose work is not manual. Once an incessant flow of information–which is more anxiety-inducing than of genuine interest–has been examined, the time available is divided between social media, messages and emails. This creates tangible tension, a state of stress, vulnerability and irritability which can lead to depression and burnout. Algorithms, whose powers of calculation are greater than ours and reduce the element of uncertainty, are in danger of making us redundant.

This online bulimia overloads the nervous system and causes genuine addiction. The kit made up of phone, tablet and laptop, not to mention smartwatches, robots and virtual personal assistants have changed a minority of the population into zombies. This leads to an even greater danger, an inevitable disconnection from one's internal clock, and from the relationship with time and nature. Going to bed reading and responding to people's latest stories and checking for new messages the moment we open our eyes have become alienating conditioned responses, turning individuals into little more than robots. The trap has snapped shut, technology wants to seize power and control people's lives, and they end up losing their powers of concentration and inner resilience. This abusive use of technology is as addictive as drugs. And if both of these are combined, they condemn their users to a mental hell.

Homo sapiens is in grave danger, threatened by the advent of the enhanced human, outwardly human but whose free will and creativity will be greatly diminished.

Thankfully, more and more people are seeking balance and harmony and taking up spiritual practices: yoga, breath work, contemplation. It is essential that the power of feelings not be reduced to mere entertainment. The freedom to take action, to feel and to choose sublimates our existence, gives meaning to our lives and conditions our relationships with others, animals, plants and the whole of creation. In this anxiety-prone society, traveling life's path with equanimity requires discipline, a raised level of consciousness, putting our priorities in order and visualizing a life plan. The spiritual man is multidimensional. He has understood the essence of existence, the presence of subtle bodies and life energies. The transformation of his life occurs when there is an opening of the heart, a search for meaning and harmonization with nature.

· 2 ·
LIFE FORCES

The perfect organization of the universe, the galaxies, our solar system, the interactions between our planet Earth and the Milky Way–all this instills in us a sense of humility and makes us lift up our eyes to contemplate the constellations, the rhythms of nature, the seasons, the water, the air, the wind and the earth. This mechanism, in operation, engendered life. Its allegorical symphony surpasses our understanding. It broadens the limits of our consciousness, awakens the senses and liberates energies.

Homer, in the *Iliad* and the *Odyssey,* had already set down the essentials when he speculated about free will, wisdom and mankind's capacity for self-determination and living in a community; in book XVII of the Iliad, he exclaims: "Would that therefore contention might be extinguished from gods and men; and anger, which is wont to impel even the very wisest to be harsh; and which, much sweeter than distilling honey, like smoke, rises in the breasts of men."

We live in a paradise, and in it we have created the conditions of hell. Respect for living things and biotopes ought to be a priority for all. Nature is not only our ally, but also the precondition for our existence. The sun fuels photosynthesis, creates oxygen, feeds the soil, rivers and oceans and regulates our lives to perfection. How has humankind reached the point where we forget that our every heartbeat, our every movement, is only possible through the energy of this minutely adjusted machine? Our biological clock is directly tuned to the cosmic pulse of the universe. Nothing happens by chance. Everything is part of a perfect and interconnected divine plan. Water possesses its own internal mechanics, trees communicate with each other, the force of the planets and the moon influences our own lives as much as those of animals and plants.

The world of the farmer has significantly contracted. The mechanization, and especially the industrialization, of the agricultural sector have sacrificed diversity on the altar of productivity and standardization. The increasing numbers of the population and the lengthening of life expectancy have increased mankind's food requirements. The reliability of harvests must be guaranteed and markets organized. This goal has been achieved, but it has not solved the problems of famine and malnutrition in poor countries and of overconsumption in the rich ones.

The best and the worst exist side by side on the surface of the globe, and mankind behaves with complete thoughtlessness, without the least sense of guilt.

But in spite of everything, it is vital to have confidence in humankind, at the center of the problems but also the provider of potential solutions.

The time has come for each of us to light our lantern and practice loving kindness towards ourselves, other people and nature, which is our most precious treasure and which we must protect for future generations, committing ourselves to respecting biodiversity on the Earth. To act in this way is a civic duty, militant, ethical and just, and it implies education, an awakening of the consciousness of each person, learning the art of living together and respecting differences.

It is not too late to heal our individual and collective neuroses and preserve the essential, so as to ensure peace and live in a serene, harmonious world. It is an essential condition, and without it we shall be called sharply to order by the universal power, when the erroneous course that we have obstinately followed is brutally corrected in chaos. In all domains, and especially agriculture, which feeds the planet, we must use the best of research and technology in the service of the climate, the soils, the diversity of seeds and varieties, which ensure that we have food of good quality, varied, healthy and environmentally friendly.

Agriculture and climate change will be the decisive issues of the next ten years and will determine the quality of life on earth. It is time to stop demonizing the community of farmers, who tend their holdings unremittingly, three hundred and sixty-five days a year, often to the point of exhaustion. The time has come to guarantee the income of farmers sustainably, in the framework of required specifications beneficial to the environment and binding on the farmer as regards the use of synthetic phytosanitary treatments: the use of chemical inputs – herbicides, fungicides and fertilizers – must be drastically limited in the next five years and in due course prohibited. This is a challenge to applied research and state governments, but is vital for water and air quality and the vitality of soils.

In parallel, it is important to reduce our consumption of meat, because the cereal and water consumption levels of cattle-raising are too great. The consumer society, the marketing industry and fast food have encouraged excessive consumption of meat and dairy products, well over the nutritional needs of an omnivorous adult person.

The next health scandal will be the consequence of pesticide residues, affecting not only human health, but also numerous species of birds, animals and insects, whose continuing disappearance is caused by these substances. The alarming deaths of bees in the industrialized, so-called 'civilized countries', should impel us to act as fast as possible in developing organic agriculture, which safeguards the life of pollinators, soil fertility and air quality. We are surrounded by a sentient and supersentient world, invisible to the naked eye of the uninitiated, on which the survival of our species depends.

For over three thousand years, wine-growing around our planet has been producing wines derived from one thousand five hundred different grape varieties. Wine does not have a vital function, and for this reason, should be exemplary. It warms our hearts, brings people together, accompanies our meals and often prides itself on its geographical origin. Wine should not taste of something, but of somewhere. It has a sacred dimension, symbolic and well loved, enabling us, wherever we are, to celebrate fellowship, friendship and the art of living.

In wine-growing, organic farming will become standard practice over the next twenty years. Consumers will want to drink more personalized products, guaranteeing traceability, character and flavor.

In wine-growing, organic farming will become standard practice over the next twenty years. Consumers will want to drink more personalized products, guaranteeing traceability, character and flavor.

The gifts of our Mother-Earth and the ingenuity of humankind have created the conditions for unbroken food supplies in all democracies. The necessity now is to generalize the conditions for sustainable agriculture, extending them to developing countries as well. Proper food is a basic need that should be guaranteed for all, like the availability and quality of water and air.

There are many foundations, associations and NGOs that have introduced monitoring and educational tools for the protection of biodiversity, oceans and soils, because the human race has caused more damage and imbalances in the last fifty years than since the creation of the universe. In the face of this unprecedented situation, it is our duty to establish a global-scale inventory in order to create a new organization in which we can live better and under less stress, respecting nature and our origins.

· 3 ·
HUMAN NATURE

There seems to be a general consensus on announcing the end of an era and the beginning of a new one. Humanity, as we have already discussed, has entered a tumultuous and frantic period. Technological advances are more rapid than the capacity of human beings to integrate them into their everyday lives. Consumer society gives almost all countries the necessary tools for the flow of information (television, computers, telephones, the Internet, video games) and unchecked hedonism (alcohol, drugs and medication), while opening the doors indiscriminately to a culture and ideology aimed at a rudderless youth, whose traditional points of reference (family, education and so on) are collapsing. Addictions are running rife and threatening to capsize the vessel we are embarked upon.

This leads us to the essential question – where are we going? What do we want? What do we seek?

Information overload, terrorism and climate change threaten our equilibrium. The current generation is running up debt that jeopardizes the quality of life of future ones. The diabolical machine is racing out of control, creating more selfishness, amplifying inequality and stirring up hatred between peoples, ethnic groups and religions, thereby encouraging tribalism and unrestrained capitalism.

Young people can no longer always tell the difference between the virtual world and the real one. Google Glass or Pokemon Go blur the distinction between the offline and online realms. Tablets have become children's best friends, the smartphone the favorite companion of parents, and social networks grandparents' best buddy. The Internet is one big party, as long as the lights are still on and sleep does not drag you into a different reality.

Mankind's vanity allows us to think we are masters of the game. If we compress the history of our planet into a single calendar year, we discover that a day is equivalent to twelve million years, that the first bacteria appeared in February, the first fish in November, the dinosaurs in mid-December, our ancestors on the afternoon of the 31st of December and our species, *Homo sapiens,* around 11.30 p.m! We are therefore but a drop in the universal ocean.

Solutions do exist that would enable the creation of a paradise on earth in which everyone could live happily while cultivating loving kindness, respect for diversity and fellowship. We must put out the fires of fear, and light the candles of love. The culture of fright, bordering on terror, is connected to that of power and control over others. It is fed by certain political regimes and is the cause of illness, neurosis, depression, envy and isolation. It is also at the root of why our current system is failing. Fear is like an echo reverberating in the human mind, and giving rise to negative thoughts that hinder fulfillment, the spiritual impulse and the awakening of the senses. Humanity has placed God on a pedestal, and many religions preach guilt rather than love: "You shall fear the Lord your God!" And yet, it is mainly in Man's state of separation from God that fear can take root.

The Jewish, Christian and Muslim religions have shared roots, and yet, in their name, we wage war between brothers and sisters. It is

Fear is like an echo reverberating in the human mind, and giving rise to negative thoughts that hinder fulfillment, the spiritual impulse and the awakening of the senses.

essential that we work towards the evolution of our levels of consciousness and tolerance by focusing on those things that bring us together rather than those which divide us. All the great ascended masters, at different periods in history, have delivered a message of love. For the span of their incarnations, these spiritual guides cultivated their divine nature and exemplified the necessity for change from within.

Our parentage, our history and culture determine whether or not we have studied or been drawn to a philosophy or religion that gives a solid foundation to our lives. Tolerance is essential, as is acceptance of differences as a positive contribution that broadens our minds. Sacred texts and revered writings have contributed to shaping our civilization and inspiring us. Religion has triggered many a war, and so the interpretation of parables, metaphors and allegories needs to be learned and explained. Hell and the devil are the fate that awaited those who did not put the precepts into practice. Wisdom would consist in creating a union with God, thereby proposing a different path that would put an end to fear and allow positive, open and generous emotions to bloom. God is omniscient, everywhere and in everything.

Humans possess the most sophisticated form of consciousness on the planet. Our vocation is to respect our neighbor, open our hearts, love fraternally and connect with nature, putting the higher common good before our own immediate interests.

After guilt and fear comes the question of death. It affects how humans behave in life, their actions and beliefs. For some, it is seen as the moment of the final tally, when one answers to God. For others, after death comes nothingness, and hence separation, grief, and the end of the human journey. We could also contemplate a more peaceful vision of our mortality, one of transition, a shift in our state of consciousness, a liberation of the spirit and soul, the end of suffering and the transferral to another plane.

To be aware of our oneness with God is to connect with the universal creative power, cosmic energy, to the pulse and rhythm of nature. We open the doors to a new state of consciousness, in which life becomes a continuous process of growth, experience, creativity, discovery, and wonder.

To connect with Mother Earth is to enter into resonance with the universe. We are multidimensional beings – our physical, etheric and astral bodies, our chakras, senses and feelings make up a complex, interactive whole, both vulnerable and powerful. The power of the mind can generate ideas that change the world. Thoughts belong to the intellectual mind and thus to the deeper self. The creative power of the universe manifests through intuition, inspiration and imagination. Bliss is the ultimate stage of enlightenment, which the great mystics have experienced.

Faith is the engine, the impulse that generates this process of creation. It has meaning only if it is experienced deeply within. It must be lived on a daily basis, not vicariously, one step at a time, journeying into the unknown without fear of risk.

God is life. To be alive is to accept that each being is unique and must carve out a path for themselves in resonance with their aspirations. When we allow universal love and the power of pure intention to carry us, the way appears of its own accord.

· 4 ·
WONDER

Imagine a morning that begins with a gentle, harmonious awakening. The first decision is to throw open the shutters and let the fresh morning air into the bedroom.

In full mindfulness, we can give thanks to creation for the new day, as it unfolds in its unique way. To watch the dawn break is to be conscious of the natural cycle which, in a perfect symphony, allows us to live, receive nourishment and connect to the universe. Through breathing and rejecting any kind of negative thought, we begin by rediscovering the miracle of life, with the soul of a child.

Let us leave our mobile phone in flight mode before it becomes the center of our attention again. Let us take a break and concentrate on our inner self and our inner temple. Our body, that prodigious, complex machine, has utilized our sleep time to regenerate, allowing our dreams and subconscious to connect to the global field. Each one of us is unique, engaged in an existential quest, and must grasp the nature of our role on this earth. To do this, positively and consciously, we must widen our mental horizon, understand the hidden meaning of things, listen to the breath of the wind, forget our ego so that our 'me' makes space for the immensity of the universe and for amazement.

Giving thanks also means accepting passing difficulties. The good news about your problems is that no one will have taken them away during the night.

It is through action that we feel alive. To accept challenges is also to comprehend that the way ahead of us presents stumbling blocks so that we can overcome them, sublimate them and in this way strengthen our creative energy, our power and our determination. "It shall be done for you as you have believed" (Matthew 8:13).

Accepting your incarnation, being aware of your uniqueness and of this opportunity that life offers is a gift, a transcendent grace. Children have the capacity to wonder every day and forget what happened the day before. Starting with a clean slate, they begin each day with a smile in the firm belief that all is well. What an adult must rediscover is not wonder, which is a concept, but the capacity to wonder.

After developing interiority and familiarizing ourselves with contemplation, we tackle the next step: meditation, revealing what is most profound and intimate within us. This aware presence creates an opening, a surge of loving kindness, respect, harmony and beauty. It is a vibratory condition, a flame that ignites positive thoughts, a love for creation that releases energy and gives us the courage to live and make decisions. By consenting to be cured of our wounds and obsessions, we open our hearts and our spirit to wonder.

Life is not a long, placid river, but it offers us the choice of freeing ourselves from our chimeras and illusions. It is an extraordinary experience for anyone who is in search of truth. When we face reality, we consent to see the marvelous in every being. It is the way that forms the beauty of existence and surprises us when we least expect it. Reality is never humdrum. It can sometimes have the best in store for us.

A positive, altruistic state of consciousness will open the gates to happiness, success and abundance. It is not more virtuous to be poor and unhappy than to be rich and happy.

In Nelson Mandela's inauguration speech, he repeatedly extolled the beauty of the world. He had sublimated suffering and transformed it into experience to become a loving person, devoid of animosity towards his jailers or resentment against his judges. His smile, his gaze and his words fill us with joy and give force to our prayers. "Our deepest fear," he said, "is not that we are inadequate. Our deepest fear is that we are powerful beyond measure. It is our light, not our darkness, that most frightens us. We ask ourselves, 'Who am I to be brilliant, gorgeous, talented, fabulous?' Actually, who are you not to be? You are a child of God. Your playing small does not serve the world. There's nothing enlightened about shrinking so that other people won't feel insecure around you. We are all meant to shine, as children do. We were born to make manifest the glory of God that is within us. It's not just in some of us; it's in everyone. And as we let our own light shine, we unconsciously give other people permission to do the same. As we're liberated from our own fear, our presence automatically liberates others."

This message, filled with love, wisdom and tolerance is a source of inspiration for all of us, especially the most destitute, those who suffer and whose everyday life is hard. Nothing is final, everything is transitory. We should always see a hidden meaning in the events of life, which are sometimes blessings in disguise. To believe in God is lucky, but to believe in oneself is a requirement. Who am I not to believe in myself? Life is not a foregone conclusion, but a battle, a quest, a winding road strewn with pitfalls.

Symbolically, we must learn to lay down the burden weighing on our shoulders and free ourselves of this load so that we can sleep the sleep of the just, the sleep of those who are certain that tomorrow belongs to them.

Every evening, when we get home and before going to bed, it is a good idea to take a few minutes for ourselves and prepare ourselves for rest. Symbolically, we must learn to lay down the burden weighing on our shoulders and free ourselves of this load so that we can sleep the sleep of the just, the sleep of those who are certain that tomorrow belongs to them. This introspection is an ascetic practice, a moment when we have clarity of vision, and a positive message that we send to ourselves and to the world. Tomorrow is another day, and the worst is never a certainty. The best is often yet to come.

The capacity for wonder is natural to the younger ones, because they are open-minded, receptive to learning and the discovery of everything around them. Naturally and unconsciously, they are building themselves day by day and developing their cognitive potential, their emotional intelligence and their relations with others in a harmonious impetus demanding no effort. For them, every day contributes to the construction of the self. Parents who favor an upbringing based on creativity, encounters and dialogue create the conditions for this blossoming. Sport is a school for overcoming fresh challenges, for solidarity, leadership and humility, which develops confidence. This positive and open mindset helps us to move forward and assimilate new data.

The rungs of the ladder of life are assembled one by one, at the cost of an effort that varies from one personality to another. We each have to find our own rhythm, whether we are children, adolescents or adults. Each path is unique, like each destiny. Abnormality is the rule. Wonder is also found in knowing ourselves, accepting our own strengths and weaknesses and forgiving ourselves for our setbacks and mistakes.

From the infinitely small to the infinitely great, man is a speck of dust in the universe, but at the same time, he is a particle of God, a living, creative flame. It is a strength, but also a requirement, to reveal ourselves to ourselves so that we can meet the challenges of each day and be happy. Day by day, the quest for the self, the comprehension and acceptance of our being, develop this inner power that generates happiness, wisdom and love.

We are unique, with a body, a consciousness, a mind and a soul which raises us up.

The hierarchy of cycles, starting from the mineral and continuing through the plant and the animal to attain the human, lays upon us a responsibility associated with our dominant position and asks us to understand, with humility, that this evolution has been made possible by a creative dynamic that has engendered the human species on this planet. What sublime organization!

Every day, we can find thousands of reasons for wonder. The first step is to be aware that we really are living beings, not just zombies drifting from place to place. It is a question of taking back control of our lives and directing our actions positively, with purpose and empathy.

The sun shines, nature bustles, the song of birds in the town or in the middle of park echoes this promise. Silence opens the door to a sweet, soothing melody. I make my choices, order my priorities. I generally devote the first thirty minutes to taking care of myself. My physical body is waking up, my breathing increases in power, depth and rhythm. My muscles are called into play, stretching and retracting harmoniously. I exist, I am awake and in tune with my deep being. I am ready to start a new day, open to the field of all possibilities. I visualize numerous positive scenes which are going to alter the course of my daily life and influence the remainder of my existence. I am in the eternal present, and I feel the energy of creation. I am unique, and I deserve the best while maintaining respect for others.

This breath of love strengthens my creative force and frees me from anxieties and fears. It enables me to feel and use this fluid, these vibrations, this oxygen. I make peace with myself, driving away the negative and destructive energy that holds me prisoner, limits me and prevents me from progressing. Attaining full awareness is a method, an intimate moment, which will help me to open up and will give me the necessary strength and love. I feel a desire to share this moment, to cry out and exult, in my family, with my relatives or friends, but even with people who don't like me. Wonder is both the cause and consequence of love. It is simultaneously subject and object. By forgiving others, we also permit ourselves this personal choice and make our way, casting aside our burdens. I feel as free as a bird, and I fly to my next triumphs. I have the soul of an adventurer: I explore new horizons and fresh frontiers. My projects are my opportunity. They depend on nobody and must be in tune with my desires. They may be personal or collective.

Finding things out, reading a book, visiting an exhibition, going to the cinema, meeting friends or going for a walk alone: there are endless things to be discovered. Doing nothing, having no goal, no objective, is forbidden. The devil finds work for idle hands, they say. Discipline creates a routine; it is training for going into action.

On the collective front, I choose to take part in the professional projects that I feel strongly about. There are always, on the one hand, the compulsory movements dictated by my professional program and, on the other hand, the freestyle options. I organize myself to be productive and in tune with my lifestyle and my aspirations. I seek out the true values of my business, its DNA, and I discover the meaning, which may be hidden, of my mission.

I like doing what is suggested to me: it sets me a goal, while giving me satisfaction. If I am unhappy, or not in synchrony with the basis and values of my project, I actively look for another one. To take risks is to permit oneself to win and sometimes lose, but always to learn and draw conclusions. "Experience is the name everyone gives to their mistakes," wrote Oscar Wilde. We always learn more from our failures than from our successes. We also have to learn to love difficult spells, because they give us the opportunity to build ourselves up and gain understanding of the meaning of life.

Succeeding also programs us for success, which favors the brave, the daring and those who do not stop at the first hurdle. "When there is no peril in the fight, there is no glory in the triumph": these lines by Pierre Corneille assert the virtues of work and strength of character. Step by step, brick by brick, we put our story together, building our house on solid, lasting foundations. The proverb, "Rome was not built in a day," puts in perspective the time required to accomplish great things and bring our work to completion.

The difference between victory and defeat is always hidden in the most minute detail. One must always give of one's best and leave the rest to providence and others. Nothing is ever irrevocably written in advance. The uncertainty of tomorrow is the greatest and most beautiful certainty. So let us sleep the sleep of the just, open our eyes full of hope and joy, be vibrant all day while feeling alive and useful, and always accept the unexpected as a chance that is offered to us on our journey.

The difference between victory and defeat is always hidden in the most minute detail.

Every talent is an offering and a marvel. We all have at least one in us. It is for us to make it bear fruit and put it to the test so that it grows and asserts itself with each passing day.

Doing nothing is laziness and self-inflicted punishment. To do is to exist, to become free, to grow and seek happiness and wonder.

So let us live life to the full!

PART II
TRANSCENDENCE

·5·
THE IMPETUS OF THE HEART

Fire burns, love transports, pain hurts, and feelings constantly arise in random succession, day after day, in the dark of the night, in our innermost selves, in communion with the cosmic pulse of the universe. The heart's impetus is strong, yet fragile, and overpowering, it may play tricks on you but will never abandon you. The heart detects essential things, guides your steps, and gives you the strength to believe and hope. It is the universal filter that drives life, animal or human, and an invisible link between all of us. It is connected to the earth and the sky, and harmonizes their pulses. It purifies the blood, regulates its flow, balances pressure and irrigates our veins, arteries and organs. It is at the center of our preoccupations and at the root of our passions and aspirations. It beats time to our inner music, and grants our desires. It senses, feels, and aligns body, mind and soul. Its shape and color symbolize love, fellowship, and hope.

When the heart opens, the unconditional love that gives faith and transcends existence is born. This brotherly bond creates osmosis, energy and emotion. The heart is both the time-bound and timeless opening onto the source of creation, the divine. It unites us and preserves us from oblivion and chaos. It makes us happy, sad, sick or well. In a single instant, it can pierce us and cause us great harm, or flood us with overwhelming love.

We lose our grip on normality if we let it take the reins of our life. We discover the beauty of each morning, the freshness of the day, the smile that beckons another. This capacity for enthusiasm is a boon, a ray of sunshine, the scent of a rose, the sound of the wind, the energy of water, the symphony of nature. The great universal orchestra keeps time with absolute perfection. Sometimes, the heart of the earth rejoices, volcanoes awaken and deposit rivers of molten lava that will remain for thousands of years. It is an ode to joy, and to love, for creation, a celebration of the living world. The heart is a gem of precision engineering, a perpetual engine, an accurate clock at the service of every being on earth. It begets emotions and, like an inner compass, guides each and every individual.

"One sees clearly only with the heart. Anything essential is invisible to the eyes." This is the secret given by the fox to the Little Prince in the story by Antoine de Saint-Exupéry. Wandering in the desert after falling from a star, it is himself that the character finds while seeking his way. It is a universal tale, an initiation into truth and love. The mind, the mental faculties, are too alienated by the ego to aspire to attaining the same level of realization. The heart is the sun in living beings. It perceives heat and energy, and it stimulates the physical body.

The heart is the sun in living beings. It perceives heat and energy, and it stimulates the physical body.

Life is fragile, and hangs always in the balance. It is unique and, potentially, unlimited other than by its shadow, death. These are the two faces of a single sphere, forever spinning and granting us an infinite cycle of renewal.

The great eras of civilization have been the milestones of human evolution. The heart of the world shifted in turn from Greece to Rome, then to the peoples of the North, Venice, Antwerp, Genoa, and more recently to America and China. The dominant region controls the world for a time which is only a brief span on the scale of humanity.

Each generation contributes to an awakening, to creativity and new organizational structures. The Renaissance was characterized by boundless imagination and an astonishing aesthetic sense. Michelangelo, Leonardo da Vinci, Raphael and others vied with each other in ingenuity, talent and genius. This unstoppable current gave birth to unique masterpieces which delight us.

Beauty comes from the heart: it does not judge or measure, but rejoices in the act of creation and of sublimating the elements, thereby revealing the soul of the artist. We all have an artistic streak. Some have been endowed with a special gift that surpasses understanding and morality. They channel their view of the world into their work, and, further, amplify the universal message. The heart of these men and women enters into absolute resonance with their soul, connected to the pulse of the universe.

The breath creates rhythm. Rhythm frees the breath. The vehicle of the body must be preserved and trained if it is to give impetus to our lives. To become aware of our oneness, of our relationship to the whole, allows us to be more open to others and to the universal matrix. We have the power to take action and to believe in an invisible force that connects us. This can be the result of a gradual awakening, at the end of a long inner journey. In some cases, a particular event, brought about by exceptional, or even dramatic circumstances, reveals our multidimensional nature. Our body, in its three dimensions – physical, energetic and emotional – is connected to our etheric and astral sheaths. We are constantly steeped in the forces of earth and cosmos that keep us upright.

The heart of our galaxy is the sun, and thanks to its continuous rays it is the enabler of life on earth. Heliocentricism, conceptualized by Copernicus and formalized by Galileo and Kepler, positions it at the center of our planetary system. The analogy between the sun and the heart of living beings reveals an interconnection of the planets with the four elements that make up the earth–mineral, plant, animal and human.

In our expanding universe, billions of different planets and systems exist. The Milky Way is a veritable mechanism interacting with the other systems and comprising a number of circulating magnetic and energy fields. This is beyond our comprehension and can be frightening for many of us. There are physicists who risked their lives in order to demonstrate fundamental truths. In 1687, Isaac Newton proposed a mathematical formula for gravitational attraction, and his laws of motion. The great prophets–Abraham, Elijah, Moses, Buddha, Jesus and Muhammad–for their part, contributed to the elevation of human nature by establishing rules, laws, and hope based on love for one's fellow humans, solidarity and transcendence. This impetus comes from the heart. The task of organizing our resilience on a global scale cannot be left to the ego and to the mind.

These legendary figures had received the teachings of their spiritual guides, and their awakening came about by their asceticism, their volition and their seeking, but especially by their capacity to reach enlightenment. It is the opening of the heart that creates this state of transition, in direct connection with God, regardless of the name given him–Yahweh, Jehovah, Allah, Zeus, Brahma, Everlasting Lord. The power of their commitment stemmed from their awareness, and grew through their actions, their preaching, the influence they had over peoples and their miraculous words as beings of light. Only a heart filled with love for all beings and freed of any fear can attain bliss. This spiritual communication, spread over the span of generations, was also practiced by philosophers such as Confucius in China or Socrates, Plato and Aristotle in Greece. Although the latter are not regarded as prophets, their wisdom, clear-sightedness and writings continue to inspire entire peoples.

The majority of religions are founded on the concept of an immortal soul, which, in some, reincarnates. Christianity identified Jesus as the son of God, who rose again and guided the apostles in their writing of the Gospels. In him also, the impetus of the heart is his creed: "Love one another" is his universal message that shines its light well beyond the confines of the church. It is the bedrock of community life, the assurance of a harmony and balance removing separation between human beings, nature and the cosmos.

Two worlds oppose each other, two sides of a single coin – on one, progress, the economy, the market; on the other, transcendence, empathy and health. One cannot exist without the other.

Humanity, in the course of its development, has reached a pivotal stage in its evolution. After all the torment, tumult and wars, it has succeeded in creating the conditions for a more conciliatory and civilized life. And yet, spirituality is under strain from materialism. Two worlds oppose each other, two sides of a single coin – on one, progress, the economy, the market; on the other, transcendence, empathy and health. One cannot exist without the other. The focus must be on the axes of priority without upsetting the subtle balance of our structures.

Man must regain his central role, not in the service of his own material needs, but in the interests of resilience and restored harmony, with himself, his fellow men and his environment.

In this 21st century, empathy has become a critical issue for humanity. Understanding the feelings of others requires an open, altruistic mind. The importance of being able to put oneself in the shoes of another is valid on an individual level, but also on a global one, since it applies to all life forms on earth. Empathy embraces shared living, respect for the living world, and an understanding of sentience and supersentience.

Progress must be in the service of life on earth, and not the other way around. It must set its course towards a new art of community life, and review the foundations of the current models of domination, to arrive at a more harmonious, supportive and loving society.

· 6 ·

THE POWER OF FAITH

Since my earliest childhood, I have felt a fervor and a connection with a higher power which supports us and helps us to act. It was in action that I found faith. It gives us the courage go forward to meet our destiny and impels us to take risks by exploring beyond the confines of existence. Setting out in quest of adventure frees us from our existential fears and the burden of our personal and family history. Faith burns inside you; with it, you lose control of normality. It is a liberator, which gives you the confidence and strength to create. Faith tests us and strengthens our beliefs. It is an initiation process, which sometimes begins in adolescence, that period of doubt when we are building our self-esteem.

Faith cannot be experienced by proxy. It is a higher power which guides us, opens the doors of knowledge and brings powerful inspiration into our lives by creating a new paradigm founded on confidence, tolerance and love. The basis of this confidence is benevolence towards oneself and others. By accepting our incarnation with its imperfections, we learn to forgive ourselves for our mistakes and failures.

The dawn of each day, each new morning, is a blank page waiting to be written with enthusiasm, courage and grace. Faith is a vehicle with which we can start each day in connection with our spirit. Through meditation, prayer or contemplation, human beings focus on their inner self, liberating energies and creative thoughts. In this state of consciousness, we can cultivate positive thinking, whatever our past difficulties may have been.

At any moment along the way, by strength of will and the opening of the heart, we can come together with the Other, creating the conditions for a productive day in tune with our thoughts. Here, two principles are in confrontation while nevertheless complementing each other: on the one hand, reason, founded on intelligence, knowledge and science and, on the other hand, faith, that breath of God revealed to humankind.

The first principle is founded on doubt, the search for truth and skepticism. The second relies on demonstrations and certitudes, sometimes temporary and in process of change. Religions develop the concept of the basic otherness of the world, of which God is the sole creator. To Socrates, Plato and Aristotle, the fathers of philosophy, faith is not metaphysics. It has no religious connotation and is founded on knowledge of the real world. Plato goes further, distinguishing the visible real world from the intelligible world, that of ideas, endowed with a superior or inferior nature.

Does life have meaning, or is it mankind that gives meaning to life?

In response to this existential question, the first theologians endeavored to link philosophy with the sacred, giving faith an intellectual and rational dimension proceeding from confidence in God. In this way, faith and confidence are the two forces of one and the same conception, constituting the structure of Greek thought.

The monotheistic religions asserted a radically different postulate, based on an all-powerful God the creator. Faith, as a higher power, is incomprehensible to mankind. It is a divine gift, an offering, a force in movement which creates, transcends and gives meaning to the organization of the universe, establishing a hierarchy of the terrestrial and celestial dimensions. Hindu and Buddhist doctrines propound the notion of karma, that is to say the substrate of actions performed during incarnation, and emphasize the possibility of attaining awakening. To the Buddha, there is no meaning to life: this state of consciousness will liberate the human being from the suffering caused by our attachments.

The long evolution of the human race, the development of cognitive and affective capacities, sedentarization and education have favored the emergence of different forms of spirituality and schools of thought. *Homo sapiens* has risen by freeing itself from basic tasks such as hunting and gathering to develop social organizations that leave room for personal development, emancipation and, more recently, democracy and self-determination. Science and physics, and more recently the development of pseudo-sciences such as parapsychology, have liberated creativity and stimulated personality.

The universal laws, also known as the laws of attraction, direct the power of the spirit as a decisive element in the mode of self-determination of each person. Human discipline and willpower, associated with cognitive techniques, have the capacity to transform negative or self-destructive thoughts into positive energies and experiences. These techniques ally the energy of the mind and the psyche with spiritual power. Visualization is employed to modify the quality of emotions and enable the energetic power of the universal laws to be felt.

The obscurantism of past ages, in Egyptian and Greek antiquity, for example, was bound up with ignorance, fear and dread of the divinities. Later on, the medieval dogma of the Church in its most forbidding guise, and more recently, Islamic radicalization, have perpetuated a form of physical and mental servitude. Nevertheless, generalized access to information, the globalization of the economy and the circulation of people and ideas have opened up a fascinating epoch for humanity. Taken individually, human beings are often optimistic, but collectively, they are subject to confusion and skepticism. In the last hundred and fifty years, mankind has cast off its fetters and caused incredible changes in life on Earth. This period is unique in the modern era. It has given rise to enthusiasm, creativity, wealth and well-being and has made possible the conceptualization of anthropology. Science, research and information have also contributed to the spread of education, culture and pleasurable living.

Artificial intelligence and the prevalence of computers have plunged us into a new era. The virtual, digitalized world threatens to constitute a challenge for human beings. Free will, reasoning and democracy are not guaranteed if people weaken their defense of sovereignty and their inalienable rights to decide and act for themselves. We have inherited freedom of speech and thought from brave individuals, determined to make a better world for future generations.

Time escapes us: it takes on a relative dimension as soon as we reach out into the universe. It is a concept that gives rhythm to our lives, confining us in the temporal and in mental atrophy.

We are reaching the end of a frenzied cycle, with nuclear power on one side and the menace of a virus on the other. Danger is everywhere and is sounding the alarm on our condition as human beings. Egoism, power, money and glory are mere vanities. Longer life spans enable us to profit more from life but will never bring us immortality.

Time escapes us: it takes on a relative dimension as soon as we reach out into the universe. It is a concept that gives rhythm to our lives, confining us in the temporal and in mental atrophy.

The present-day leisure society has exacerbated the individualist lifestyle based on work and travel. The space left for spiritual awakening needs to be reconsidered and regenerated. The crisis in traditional faith, founded on the practice of worship, is weakening some religions, especially in the so-called developed countries. Spiritual fervor persists in Africa and South America. In China, the Confucian world view has been superseded by individualism and a fanatical determination to succeed professionally.

Worldwide, people are interconnected and informed in real time of what the outer world provides. This communicative bulimia has altered human behavior and developed impulsive, baseless reactions. Addiction to the digital media and their vast catalogues of services destroys all force of intention and leaves behind it only conditioning and force of habit. The light embodied in the philosophers and scientists–Voltaire, Rousseau or Newton–and the transcendent divinity revealed by religions are threatened by the twilight of enslavement to the conventional wisdom.

Human beings cannot abandon freedom as a sacrifice on the altar of security. Only a spiritual awakening can give us the strength to escape from the current sclerotic, depressing torpor, bound up with lockdown in many countries and with the fear peddled by certain media. We must call ourselves into question, individually and collectively, regarding the meaning of our life on earth, our rights as citizens and our duty towards nature and future generations.

Looking beyond life on Earth, the question of our multidimensionality is vital. Materialism deadens human nature and nurtures greed, arrogance and short-term solutions. Spirituality nurtures spiritual communion, solidarity and the long-term view. Today's economic systems based on the market have shown their limitations. A long period of inactivity resulting from the coronavirus has been enough to engender a transitory recession.

The human being has become the slave of a system, the prisoner of a chimera that he himself has created.

The crisis of 2008 was insignificant compared to 2020. Human beings must once more take their place at the center of activity and be the focus of concern for all of us. It is true that since the end of World War II, we have enjoyed a golden age during which liberation of morals, circulation of goods and services and innovation have grown exponentially. The emergence of a middle class was the assurance of a sustainable system. But in the last few years, we have witnessed a concentration of capital and the erosion of the middle classes. Danger threatens and nations are disoriented, because the speed and violence of the changes have been such that people have not had time to adapt. Happiness, serenity and progress have been replaced by anxiety, insecurity and fear of what tomorrow may bring. The pressure on individuals is huge. It is the duty of visionary business managers to reassure their teams, train them continually and help them to take a holistic view of their occupation.

It is the duty of visionary business managers to reassure their teams, train them continually and help them to take a holistic view of their occupation.

Only with spiritual awakening, and a new awareness of our deep being in harmony with the meaning of our existence, can stable equilibrium and lasting joy in life be attained. This is the fundamental task for all who seek to understand their mission here on Earth, the significance of their actions and the force of their thinking.

At the height of ancient Greek civilization, debates were encouraged, leading to verbal jousting, some of which was recorded by Plato and

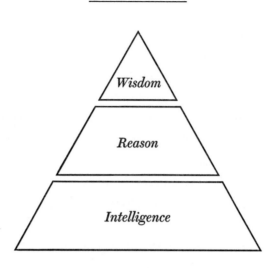

• STRUCTURE OF THOUGHT •

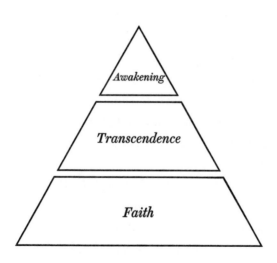

• SPIRITUAL BREAKTHROUGH •

others and survives to this day. Important questions were asked: trying to answer them demanded reflection on reason, truth and the principle of liberty. These days, immediate answers are expected, leaving no time for reasoning or debate. Our period functions at the speed of bytes and data-processing programs. The only tangible and effective response to this frenzy comes by developing intuition and connection with the universal power. Mental power must make way for a new state of mind, connected to the divine plane. This transformation means letting go and giving up outmoded systems of thought.

We must become one with the soul of the world if we want to live happy and in full awareness.

Nature is stronger and more intelligent than we are. She renews herself and will take back control sooner or later. Increasing numbers of human beings are seeking change, as they do not want to live any longer in the sidereal vacuum associated with having rather than being.

The Book of Daniel in the Old Testament describes events that began in the reign of Nebuchadnezzar, King of Babylon in 605 BCE. Daniel, known as a wise man, is summoned to interpret the king's dreams. He asks to be given time and prays God to grant him favors. The following night, his wish is granted and the secret of the dreams is revealed to him.

Daniel prepares to unveil the future of the Empire, but also to give a glimpse of world events in the coming millennia:

"You, O king, were looking and behold, there was a single great statue; that statue, which was large and of extraordinary splendor, was standing in front of you, and its appearance was awesome. The head of that statue was made of fine gold, its breast and its arms of silver, its belly and its thighs of bronze, its legs of iron, its feet partly of iron and partly of clay. You continued looking until a stone was cut out without hands, and it struck the statue on its feet of iron and clay and crushed them. Then the iron, the clay, the bronze, the silver and the gold were crushed all at the same time and became like chaff from the summer threshing floors; and the wind carried them away so that not a trace of them was found. But the stone that struck the statue became a great mountain and filled the whole earth." (Daniel 2:31-35)

The golden period represents the Babylonian empire, which collapsed in 539 BCE and was replaced by the Median-Persian power, which remained dominant until 331 BCE, then by Alexander the Great, creating the great Greek kingdom which lasted until the arrival of the Romans, thirty years before our era.

The Roman system lasted a long time before it gave way to Anglo-American domination, starting in the 18th century. The two World Wars and the economic development of China, Europe and Russia have divided the world and distributed influence and political power among nations. The image of the feet of iron and clay symbolizes the present-day division of the governments of the planet and the mistrust of the peoples for their elected representatives.

This deep-seated existential crisis and the doubt engendered by climatic, economic and political disturbances create tensions and cause introversion, authoritarianism and generalized apprehension. We are heading straight for disaster if we do not change and create a new paradigm. Humanity must assert and reinvent itself so as to create equitable, resilient living conditions for all peoples and individuals. This is an unprecedented challenge.

The Covid-19 crisis restores our humility: it proves that we are indeed a colossus with feet of clay, as Daniel prophesied. The response to this difficult but exciting period depends on the spiritual development of humanity and the acquisition of an awareness of the meaning of life, as opposed to materialism.

We do not own anything: we are at most custodians for a limited time. The planet that hosts us and offers us its wonders is alarmed by our disrespectful attitude to living things. The suicidal headlong rush, the temptation of immediate profit, the galloping consumption of fossil fuels and the relocation of all sorts of activities are stirring up trouble in our centuries-old social organization.

The aggressiveness of our decision-making systems, the dehumanization of the workplace and the crisis of governance contribute to disorienting our decision makers and favor short-termism, whereas life is a long-distance race. The stock exchange, NASDAQ, the CAC 40 and the City of London have forced capital to adhere to a three-month rhythm, which is not always consonant with a long-term vision. Attempts to induce the CEOs of groups quoted on the stock exchange to boost their ratings and please their shareholders cause decisions to be made that are sometimes in opposition to the interests of the companies concerned and their employees.

Of course, an ideal world is a utopia, because the human spirit, the need for self-assertion and the will to conquer will always keep the hungriest appetites alive. However, some form of regulation will be used to keep this unrestrained world in check, giving energy and resonance to generous spirits to create a safer, more just and more stable world.

This better world will be genuinely spiritual, seeking to build awareness of our multidimensionality and to open people's hearts.

May it be so.

· 7 ·
BEING MULTIDIMENSIONAL

To this day, the process of creation of the universe remains a mystery which researchers have tried to explain by providing partial answers of varying coherence. Two schools contend with each other: one which leaves the mystery part to God, and that of the atheists or agnostics, which rests on the Big Bang theory. Planck came close to grasping the moment the universe was created and began its never-ending expansion. Enlightened human thought recognizes that such perfect harmony and astonishing organization surpass our understanding and intelligence.

The intellect separates humans from animals. Consciousness and language confer on humans extraordinary but unequal abilities depending on the person. The size of the brain, over a period of more than four hundred thousand years since the Neanderthal age, has grown considerably resulting in behavioral changes. First of all, it took mankind a long time to get upright and go from being on all fours to a balanced standing posture on two feet. Subsequently, the mastery of fire, the settling of families, and the discovery of farming made possible tremendous advances. Life became organized around communities and humans pursued their process of evolution, developing their thinking and memorization abilities. Rules of living, albeit rudimentary ones, emerged, as did the celebration of rites and traditions, and instinct is what guided mankind's actions. He was a primitive being, endowed with a very limited degree of intelligence. Over the course of a very gradual evolution, human beings learned to live a secure life by obtaining their sustenance from hunting, gathering and harvesting.

Towards the end of the Paleolithic age, humans developed the power of intention. This was the beginning of reasoning, planning, formulating ideas and the relationship to time. Intention asserts willpower, conviction and personality. Tautavel man, discovered and studied by Henri and Marie-Antoinette de Lumley, dates back to the Acheulean period of the lower Paleolithic age, or five thousand years before our time. Research carried out by their teams has brought to light the consecutive organizational models of the first men.

The development of intelligence brought about an evolution of humans who began, inexorably, to understand universal processes, their relationship to the elements–earth, water, fire–the presence of the moon in the sky, and the existence of the cosmos. The rhythm of the seasons, the path of the sun, waiting for the rains and so on, gave birth to rituals and beliefs. In this way, man passed through the gateway of the mind, and this revealed to him his own multi-dimensionality. He improved his sensory and conscious abilities.

Intelligence structures a human being, and gives content to reasoning, theory and demonstration. Every person's abilities are different, but, just like muscles, they can be kept well-functioning, in particular through learning. Some people are more gifted than others at birth, and have higher potential. In our modern societies, intellectual capabilities are a criterion for detection and selection, and serve to direct young people towards specific careers.

An awareness of ability, associated with proven determination, creates people with extremely high potential. The intellectual mind is the cornerstone of our evolution and it opens the doors to transcendence: It has assumed a predominant position and sometimes has a tendency to want to govern the affairs of the world.

The balance between different kinds of intelligence is subtle. We know that specific functions pertain to each hemisphere of the brain:

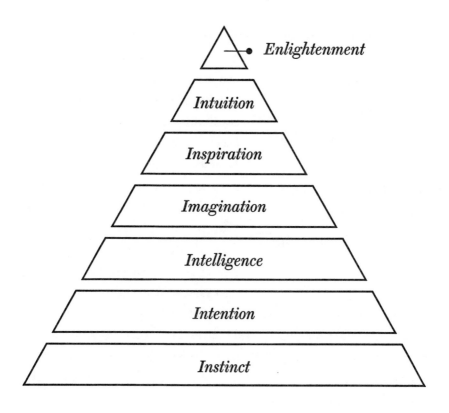

• PYRAMID OF TRANSCENDENCE •

logic and rationality to the left brain, synthesis and intuition to the right. "Left brainers" are more active in, and excel at, being analytical, inquisitive and methodical, while struggling at times to disconnect from their minds. "Right brainers" for their part find it easier to disengage from the intellectual mind by trusting their feelings. They are naturally more inclined to give free rein to their thoughts and look ahead. The *corpus callosum* (callosal commissure) establishes the connection between the two hemispheres and enables mental harmony.

To open the door on one's inner being, on one's capabilities and shortcomings, is a courageous act and the first step towards the release of energy and potential.

On the basis of each person's capabilities, it is important to discern their intrinsic qualities concisely. Equilibrium consists in reinforcing one's strengths and minimizing one's struggles, to maximize one's potential. This purposeful approach requires, first of all, an individual shift in awareness. It is effective if something clicks between the ages of twenty and thirty-five, when the person is mature enough to integrate the I, the caretaker of their uniqueness and individuality. This is a path that can be followed alone, in empirical fashion, relying on observation, feeling and introspection. Personality tests can be helpful if they assess skills and highlight individual abilities.

To open the door on one's inner being, on one's capabilities and shortcomings, is a courageous act and the first step towards the release of energy and potential. Education within the family circle may be incomplete, but in most cases it constitutes a springboard from which personality can take off after adolescence. For the Lebanese poet Khalil

Gibran, education consists in preparing children to leave the nest:

> *Your children are not your children.*
> *They are the sons and daughters of Life's longing for itself.*
> *They come through you but not from you,*
> *and though they are with you yet they belong not to you.*

The Prophet, chapter IV.

Each person does what they can with greater or lesser success. Once adulthood is reached, it becomes a duty to take stock, and assess what has been learned from school and family, and identify the areas that need more work to become a better person. This structuring process, which takes a few years, heals wounds and fears and sometimes neurosis.

Emotional intelligence applied with conscious awareness is unsurpassed for a successful life. In contrast, when the ego is still the guide, it produces people lacking sensitivity and empathy, who direct their dull lives towards a material ideal. Intelligence in the service of humanity facilitates the pathway between mind and spirit but also between the finite and infinite universes.

Today's world, thrown wide open, is facing new issues which cannot be resolved by outworn patterns of thinking. A new life template for planet Earth must be conceived.

For Freud, the interpretation of dreams is the royal road leading to knowledge of the subconscious. In sleep, the mind steps aside for our dream state. It projects us into the subconscious part of our being and connects us to an extrasensory world. In order to assess the value of a dream, we can ascertain its nature. According to the Arab historian Ibn Khaldun, there are three kinds of dreams: those that come from God, those that come from angels, and those emanating from the devil.

"Clear dreams are divine in origin. Allegorical dreams emanate from angels. And confused dreams are demonic in origin, because they are vain and Satan is the root of vanity." In the same way, writers and the great Christian mystics, right up to the present day, agree upon the different states. Modern psychology, for its part, has introduced the concept of rapid eye movement sleep in order to differentiate the various stages of dreams and make them easier to identify. "If there be a prophet among you, I the Lord will make myself known unto him in a vision, and will speak unto him in a dream." (Numbers 12:6).

Socrates, Plato and Aristotle wrote about dreams, their origins and their meanings. Time and time again, Homer used dreams to describe communication between the gods and humans. Shamans, too, give great importance to dreams, and seek to enter this state of consciousness through sacred rituals. They have put forward, just as the ancient Egyptians had, the idea of a personal double for each person. During sleep, the soul-spirit is said to have the ability to leave the earthly body in order to reconnect with its double and receive premonitions, messages enabling it to pursue its journey and which give form to new ideas.

Far from being limited to dreams, daydreams and visions, the imagination, according to Aristotle, calls upon intelligence. For Rudolf Steiner, in the spiritual world, a gaze becomes imagination and develops clairvoyance, which occupies a central position in the pyramid of transcendence of man, as it establishes the connection between mind and spirit, reason and the divine. Spirituality will spread if humanity opens its heart to a generous and altruistic urge. Access to this impulse can be unlocked by means of conscious education and a desire for autonomy.

Imagination expresses itself in the realm of time. Saint Augustine describes it by distinguishing reproduction (the present), imitation (the past) and prefiguration. With mindfulness, human beings can perceive a present image and reproduce it. Imitation is a process rooted in memory. From the ability to anticipate comes the emergence of concepts, ideas or countenances that foreshadow what might happen.

Imagination stimulates creativity and inventiveness. The artists of the Renaissance–poets, painters and sculptors–contributed to this movement, which symbolizes the transition from a dark and morbid period to a current of enthusiasm and creative forces. This impetus can be developed during the day (lucid dreaming) or in a state of heightened sensitivity. Everybody possesses a remarkable level of sensitivity that can be activated by silence, meditation, prayer or a state of mindfulness. Some, endowed with highly developed sensors, pick up effortlessly on things. They can foretell phenomena and the coming trends of the planet and our society, and, on a more intimate level, the evolution of the human soul.

It is clear that the 21st century marks the beginning of a new cycle, the shift from relentless and materialistic individualism to a movement of peace, love and harmony upheld by the younger generation. We are witnessing an astonishing and violent clash of generations. *Millennials* and the people currently in power clearly do not have the same priorities. The entrance to this new era, which is essential for the planet, will be conceptualized by the young people reaching adulthood today. They are inspired by new organizational structures which promote a circular economy and a reduction of our carbon footprint, and driven by a need for solidarity and well-being. Present-day inequalities do not allow these concepts to spread widely, nor even the establishment of an order of priorities. This is a new process springing from a more spiritual dimension. The attainments of the new generations will be fueled by compassion, which transcends one's own life and participates in the lives of others.

We are seeing a turnaround in trends: extreme egoism and selfishness will be replaced by strong shared values emanating from a higher level of consciousness. This is a profound and fascinating evolution, which will produce lasting change in people's priorities. The fight between the old world and the new has begun.

The progress in the past hundred years on an economic, social, cultural and educational level, but also in science, research, and the understanding of the universe, has been remarkable. Now, at the end of this period, we have nevertheless consumed more energy than all previous generations put together and have reached, or perhaps even passed, the limits beyond which the survival of our species becomes threatened: rampant population growth, longer life expectancies, increased exploitation of the planet's resources. Nature is quite clearly suffering from human activities. Mankind must return without delay to a harmony with ecosystems without which disasters such as fires, droughts, water shortages, heat waves, tsunamis and tornadoes will occur more and more often.

Moreover, catastrophes fuel the inequalities between the wealthy few and the rest of humanity. We live today in an open, connected world, but one which is increasingly tough and aggressive for the weakest and most deprived among us.

Every human being has a right to pure air and safe, clean water. But even these two fundamental needs are not necessarily met—in too many countries water is scarce, and sometimes unfit for human consumption. In big cities, pollution and spikes in temperature generate poor quality air.

Admittedly, it is possible, at minimal cost, to use one's tablet or smartphone. Such progress keeps people informed and facilitates the dissemination of the principles of democracy. It is nevertheless a pity that the connection to a machine and to the universal matrix—the Internet, the virtual world—has sometimes replaced feeling the forces of nature—the real world.

Finding balance once again, awakening to the beauty of the world is an authentic act which gives deep meaning to life and puts priorities in order. Humankind can reactivate its capacity to connect with higher forces, those that govern the Earth and the solar system. If we are willing to open the doors of our minds to the supernatural, inspiration will be given us by the breath of God which guides us. We all need a transcendent impulse and to be sticklers for truth. Man is not a machine—he must not become an enhanced human or a robot.

We must ask ourselves, urgently, those questions relating to our presence on earth and the goal of our lives, if we are to find wholeness.

Intelligence and reason have given us manners in ways of behaving and being. The salvation of mankind, the alpha and the omega of our lives, the creed, require knowledge of the essential truths revealed by the message of God. Writing the verses of the Bible, the early scribes were inspired by and connected to this supernatural power. Their rapture allowed them to go beyond what they knew, and transcribe the word of the divine. The breath of the Holy Spirit touched them. Over the centuries, many writers have received this same cosmic energy. Prophecies have been inspired by this phenomenal power – Ezekiel, in the 6th century BCE, announced the destruction of Tyre and Sidon, which took place in the year 1300 of our time. Numerous others also materialized. Divine inspiration is a source of truth. Clear and transparent, it defines human beings' principles. It guides their steps along a liberating initiatory journey, carrying hope for a better future.

Intuition, connected to the Whole, reinforces this faculty. It does not pass through the filters of analysis or reasoning. It is immediate and releases creative energy. It gives access to an accurate portrayal of the world and to feelings which render truth sacrosanct. It is not misleading, and enables man to validate a thought process or the appropriateness of a decision to be made. It is spiritual in nature, connected to the soul of each person. This idea was defended by Plato, in contrast with Epicurus who connected it to the body. According to Descartes, "There is no other path available to man to arrive at knowledge of the truth than obvious intuition and necessary deduction."

Intuition is the very essence of things.

It requires a strict practice, a spiritual preparation which, alone, can create conditions favorable to the revelation of truth and the path to follow.

It is the root of enlightenment, the culmination of a spiritual path that can be reached once free of the ego and connected with one's entire being to the divine.

Enlightenment leads to rapture of the soul. All the great masters and the great mystics – Moses, Elijah, the Buddha, Jesus, Muhammad – experienced this bliss, this deep joy, this opening of the heart, this feeling of completeness, this faith that shakes us to the core and gives access to a new birth and a sense of eternity.

PART III

THE LIBERATION OF FEELINGS

· 8 ·
BECOMING FREE OF FEAR

Fear is an emotion that manifests itself, in different degrees of intensity, as caution, mistrust, apprehension, alarm, phobia, anxiety, fright, panic, nightmare, horror, terror, psychosis, paranoia or delirium.

These words describe transient or permanent states familiar to animals and all living beings right up to the entire ecosystem.

The medieval Dark Ages, the product of ignorance, poverty and the hegemony of a system of beliefs, inculcated lasting mechanisms bound up with this generalized condition. They can be traced back further in the societies of antiquity and even in prehistory, which cultivated all sorts of phobias related to natural phenomena: fire, storms and other disasters. Bit by bit, the improvement in living conditions and an understanding of the world have helped to banish collective fears.

Nearly everywhere, present-day societies are the result of struggles waged to obtain laws or decrees, such as the French *Declaration of the Rights of Man and of the Citizen* in 1789. This decisive advance opened up a new way forward. Subsequently, the 19th century marked an important turning point in the consideration accorded to individuality and the respect of basic rights for all.

During this period, access to agricultural produce, industrialization and the development of infrastructures nurtured a liberating surge.

Safety improved and well-being became a lasting concept. Each passing day, year and decade has confirmed this blossoming and given the human race a new impetus. This trend has included individuals in all their diversity–of race, gender, color, tradition, culture, religion or ethics–to create conditions that favor personal development and the liberation of peoples. By stimulating the human spirit, it has opened the gates to a new era.

Coal-generated energy and electricity opened up new horizons and created unprecedented needs, but the First World War interrupted this momentum in Europe, leading to a resurgence of darkness. At first it was believed that this had been the war to end all wars, but nations soon discovered that security and peace were fragile and ephemeral states. Then the great stock-market crash of 1929 and the Second World War thrust us back into depression. The vulnerability of our institutions and of the banking system temporarily got the better of people's aspirations to higher standards of living.

The mechanisms of domination by totalitarian regimes took control of part of the Western world, while throughout the post-war boom years, the concept of democracy struggled to assert itself and develop. The rebuilding of the countries ravaged by the war and the movement of people and information favored the emerging need for individual liberty. May 1968 in France and Woodstock in the United States are emblematic, symbols of a desire to be freed from existing systems of thought, now too oppressive to be borne any longer. To come to be oneself, to exist, to feel that sensation of liberation, especially for women–these were the starting point for individual and collective emancipation. The universal right to vote, the opening up of Eastern Europe and the spread of democracy engendered modes of living embracing modernity, personal development, hedonism and religious freedom. America established its world leadership, China awoke, Europe substantially enlarged its frontiers and East European countries freed themselves from Soviet control. Admittedly, some countries, such as North Korea and the Philippines, remained resistant to notions of progress and individual liberty, but globally, progress was significant.

For the last fifty years, circulation of goods, services and information has been steadily developing. Most of us have our basic needs met. Education, access to culture, improved working conditions and equality of the sexes are changing behavior in our society. Deep-seated collective fears, the dogmas of conventional wisdom, destitution and poverty are making way for growth, well-being and continuous information, but also for the appearance of a form of nihilism. Since modern man sees himself as opposed to the world of the past, traditional family values, respect for institutions, the academic vision of our organizations and prescriptive modes of thought have been superseded by individualism, sexual liberation, the dictatorship of money and a crisis of faith. At this stage of our evolution, everything should set us free from fear, but what is the true state of affairs?

We are living in an Iron Age, harsh and demanding, which breeds aggressive behavior, anxiety and stress. Fear is coming to the surface again in all its forms and creating conditions favorable to the reappearance of autocratic regimes with ideologies based on a dualist vision of good and evil. International terrorism in its ideological form intensifies this feeling of fear. That is indeed its purpose, because the disproportionate reactions of states and the excessive media coverage of events offer it a free global communication campaign positioning a mere hundred or two people on the checkerboard of terror. If we reacted calmly and with greater restraint, we would be able to combat the problem more effectively and put it out of action for good.

The complexity of human nature, the deeper meaning of life, transcendence, the desire for transparency, the ideal of truth, the fear of oblivion, life after death, loss of biodiversity, global warming, the population bomb – these are among the subjects that demand our attention every day, sowing doubt in our minds and calling into question our habits, beliefs and priorities. Psychology and psychiatry can indeed offer some answers to our neuroses and psychoses, but the growth of individualism in our society, single-parent families and isolation from the family circle have exacerbated this feeling of insecurity and the palpable resulting tension.

Competition is omnipresent. There are increasing numbers of winners, but also of losers and social rejects. The media hype surrounding contemporary heroes, whether sports champions or politicians, company executives, artists or philanthropists, creates icons and exemplars. Personalities become brands launching global marketing campaigns to sell an idea, goods or services.

In our affluent society, this model of unbridled consumerism reinforces our desires and demands, developing frustrations generated by envy, the need to compare ourselves with others and feel we have the approval of the community. We are witnessing standardization of tastes, mentalities and tools as our conduct becomes more uniform. It is increasingly difficult to be different, to express our own personalities and break out of the mold imposed by the globalized world. The craving for thrills is sometimes satisfied by drugs. Cannabis, cocaine and heroin are freely available, making light of prohibitions. Being constantly called into question and subjected to the ongoing promotion of new products disturbs people who hunger for recognition. The needs generated by advertising, from our earliest youth, have developed the desire to belong to a standardized, conformist club. Cristiano's latest shoes, Kim's outfit, Rihanna's makeup, Naomi's jeans and Antoine's new smartphone are already on the online shopping list, needing only the final click to arrive on our doorstep tomorrow morning. The satisfaction derived from this standardization and this continual rebooting of our appearance give a personal pleasure that has a perverse effect: it is an element in a sort of collective hysteria that develops an addiction to social standardization and, surreptitiously, to loss of the concept of individuality.

The identity crisis lies at the heart of the problems of the 21st century.

It is for us as human beings to choose between conformism, conditioning and alienation on one hand, or the alternative, taking charge of our own lives, neutralizing negative emotions and deprogramming individual and collective fears.

Yet men and women have struggled, sometimes at the risk of their lives, to achieve a fairer, more equitable society and the right to control our own destiny. It is for us as human beings to choose between conformism, conditioning and alienation on one hand, or the alternative, taking charge of our own lives, neutralizing negative emotions and deprogramming individual and collective fears.

Fear and violence are responses to complex psychological phenomena and act differently on each person. Life is a long quest for those who decide to cast aside their demons and seek a new path, taking care of their inner being and their beauty. This search for confidence is a path strewn with pitfalls, an existential urge focusing on the meaning of life, the complexity of our incarnation, liberation from the ego, management of our emotions and taking control of our thoughts.

To improve our knowledge and make our daily lives easier, technology must be at our service without intruding. We must all learn to set our own limits and acquire the necessary discipline and rigor of conduct. This is a noble and fundamental undertaking to reconnect us with the divine wellspring within each of us, for the sovereign human is one who seeks spiritual uplift to attain self-knowledge. Because of our multidimensional nature, with a physical, spiritual and mental body, and through our hearts, the center of our personality, we can embody the universal consciousness of the Earth. To achieve harmony with our deeper nature, each of us can discover the mysteries of our existence for ourselves. Sovereignty is the basic right to decide our own path in full consciousness and in accordance with the highest principles and values. This liberating purification is attained through redefining the transcendent principles of life: education, religion, teachings. The quest for the self demands humility and a new, liberating, creative force. It comforts the ego and engenders a new, resilient energy that helps us to recover our lost power, in accordance with our words and actions.

We possess free will: it is our duty to make our own decisions, deprogramming our inner hell that we ourselves have created. We must channel our will before permitting the emergence of the unsuspected life forces that reside in us. Deprogramming fear is an essential step on the way to a better understanding of the living world and our own universal origins.

By opening this door, we become masters of our destiny and endow our lives with true meaning.

· 9 ·
DECIDING TO BE HAPPY

Happiness is not a formatted idea or concept. To be happy is an action, a long process of integration of different parameters, some of which we have control over and are modifiable. From our earliest childhood, happiness comes into our life like a mirage, an illusion, a distorted reflection of reality. Parents, and in particular a loving mother with whom the closest of bonds is shared, create conditions favorable to an infant's blooming. The first words in life are a concentrate of all that adults desperately seek–love, smiles, attention, affection, confidence, closeness, care of the body, a feeling of fulfillment and protection. For the majority of children, the foundations of happiness are laid. What is it that happens later for it to evaporate, and be lost so quickly in the whirlpool of life?

In his great wisdom, Confucius in the 5th century BCE. had established spiritual guidelines for happiness. This philosopher taught his disciples family values, self-knowledge and an understanding of life in all its diversity. He defined family and filial piety as the bedrock of a successful and well-managed education, establishing a framework around universal values such as honesty, love, willingness to help others, respect, forgiveness and responsibility.

Beyond this common frame of reference, it is essential to understand the uniqueness of every human being, each one endowed with specific physical, psychological and mental faculties and a unique personality. Two children raised by their parents in an identical manner, will reveal different character traits and affinities which will be strengthened in early adolescence and later, when the time comes to make the choices that condition life and a professional career.

During childhood, adolescence and then youth, personality is fashioned, talents and potential come to light and the first life itineraries begin. The transition to adulthood occurs between the ages of eighteen and twenty-five, when the first responsibilities and important decisions appear. A new era then begins, and the sense of happiness is shaken – it is a time of soul-searching and self-questioning. It modifies the order of priorities, particularly within our modern society. Social conquest and the will to find one's place in the professional world lead to stress, tension and doubt. This period can last several decades.

Ambition, volition, power, money and family are the key elements of a successful social and professional life. Exceptional circumstances such as the loss of a loved one, illness or failure of any kind can provide the opportunity, albeit unasked for, to reflect on one's course in life. It is in times like this that the music of happiness begins to make itself heard, and that the true questions about life arise, requiring answers.

To contemplate happiness is to look back on the path traveled with serenity and acceptance. This requires experience and a certain amount of foresight.

Often, between forty and fifty, becoming aware of the finiteness of earthly existence, a person will begin a new, more personal chapter of their life. This pivotal period begins with a redefining of our inner lives. The search for meaning becomes an urgent and vital need. "Your second life begins when you understand that you have only one," wrote Lao-Tzu. This temporary and sometimes temporal opening plunges a person into a whirlpool, a mental vortex that reinforces doubt and anxieties. Due to the pressure our aggressive and competitive world exerts on us, depression can set in also. This is an opportune moment to open the doors of a rebirth by exploring the deepest recesses of our soul and, relieved of the burden of incarnation, by connecting with a supersentient universe. This liberating journey often happens at night, because dreams offer a glimpse of spaces both unknown and sometimes premonitory.

What is happiness?

Parents are the guides for the first part of life, society generates the second, and self-knowledge reveals what potential to explore. There is no love, only proof of love. There is no such thing as happiness, only the state of being happy. Happiness has a purpose only if one feels alive, if the individual becomes aware of their incarnation and existential quest. Happiness exists because it is transient. It has meaning only because it can come and go without warning. It is less dependent on reality than on our own expectations. There is no magical formula. Happiness is the path. There is no conflict here with suffering, which can sometimes be liberating and lead to solace and a feeling of happiness. Physical action and pushing one's limits create endorphins which stimulate joy and even fulfillment.

We cannot change our bodies. The body is our temple, our incarnation. We must take care of it and listen to it, at the same time knowing how to tell the difference between transient biorhythms and lasting life forces. The power of the mind interacts with it. Moods will pass, while deep convictions guide us and show us the way.

Mankind is tremendously complex. Thought is life's engine. It knows both otherness and detachment, and thereby gives us access to a form of wisdom. The question of our relationship with others is fundamental in becoming self-aware and projecting oneself into the future. We are all interconnected by thought, which reveals the concept of individual freedom. Positive thinking demands self-discipline and effort on a daily basis, to stimulate willpower and mental power. Mankind can choose to live with intent by the power of the mind.

Life principles have their root in education and experience, and are reinforced by affirming one's identity, the deeper I. This vital spark is a boon and a blessing for those who feel a burning energy that carries their life further.

The mind-body-soul trinity, aligned on a single plane, requires an extracorporeal opening on the universe. Each chakra is a junction of channels that create this opening and well-being. Hindus, and subsequently Buddhists, identified and defined these energetic crossroads and attributed symbols to them. The Taoists, by locating and studying a network of meridians dotted with reflex points that crisscross our bodies and connect us to the cosmic environment, developed a know-how of therapeutic uses. Some Christian or Jewish schools of thought, such as the Rosicrucians or the Kabbalists, also identified this system of connection between the forces of the cosmos and the earth. The chakra energy centers are represented by disks or wheels radiating like the sun. Linked from bottom to top, they are located at the level of the perineum, the sacrum, the navel, the heart, the throat, the optic chiasm (third eye), and the fontanel.

If we attempt to understand the subtle functioning of the human body and the influences related to mental activity and the mind, we embark upon an extraordinary sensory journey. Man acts and interacts with impulses from the cosmos, the stars, electromagnetic fields, other living beings and nature. This global ecosystem is constantly modified by human activity and thoughts. Negative thoughts are caused by neurosis, unease, grudges and envy. They cause physical and psychological dysfunction of varying degrees of gravity. Everyone is unique and carries within them a creative power, a current of life, which echoes out into the universe. This cosmic pulse connects us to Gaia, mother earth, our source of nourishment.

Becoming aware of these natural and spiritual phenomena reinforces our individuality and clarifies our true identity. This interpersonal journey of initiation is at the heart of the idea of happiness. Profound happiness is not possible without having delved deeply into the origins of our incarnation and analyzed the mechanisms of the mind that shape our personality.

Sooner or later, we must conduct an initial review of our years of life, revisit our beliefs and rites, sort them, and become able to grow in awareness and power. This identity quest, this desire to harmonize our own microcosm with the macrocosm, assists the transition to the spiritual awakening that leads to the state of full awareness.

Love, intense joy and well-being are attributes of happiness but in no way do they guarantee a continuous state. Suffering, hardships and failures are the other side of the mirror, adding meaning and spice to life. They are an integral element in the construction of the self and contribute to the quest for a better life.

Modern society, the demographic explosion and unbridled use of resources, as well as, more recently, global warming and technological progress are upsetting the established balance and disrupting human activities. Humankind has always felt the need to create and achieve greater freedom by working towards better standards of living for each new generation. In the space of five hundred years, we have freed ourselves from obscurantism and developed knowledge, individual conscience, freedom of expression, affirmation of identity, and the guarantee of well-being and improved living.

The arrival of the Internet smashed to smithereens the structure of contemporary society. States are giving way, slowly but inexorably, to hegemonic groups without borders which, around new technologies, are changing life with unprecedented speed.

There is still time to collect ourselves and create the conditions for alchemy between individual and collective happiness that guarantees personal fulfillment for each one of us and survival to the human community. The materialism of our present-day society is not in alignment with the sentience and supersentience of human beings. The path must be one of empathy and respect for others and the planet. The mechanisms of domination will sooner or later have to be erased in favor of an environment more conducive to loving kindness, harmony, peace and love.

The materialism of our present-day society is not in alignment with the sentience and supersentience of human beings. The path must be one of empathy and respect for others and the planet.

From theory to practice and from concept to reality, happiness must be experienced and practiced. To be happy is to live, and to do. In action or in contemplation, a sense of completeness is attained by raising one's level of consciousness. Strong souls have the discipline and diligence not to wallow in self-pity over their worries and problems, but to overcome these by finding good reasons to sublimate and transcend their daily experience. In this way, a threshold is crossed, which opens up new perspectives and gives added impetus that guides our steps and makes us light the way for those who do not see.

Life is a test. It requires courage, effort and compassion. "A life is worth nothing, but nothing is worth a life," Malraux used to say.

To be happy can also be an act of surrender when we take care of the weak and needy. Being useful makes the heart sing and gives meaning to one's involvement. Activity revitalizes us and gives us all energy. It is an invisible thread that mutually ties people, creating connection and certainties. To be happy is to have the strength to command one's fate, the capacity for enthusiasm in times of hardship as much as in moments of grace or fulfillment. Happiness must be acquired and nurtured on a daily basis. It is the way of those who fully accept their incarnation without complaint.

Getting to know oneself is an imperative, a practice requiring diligence and the urge to explore the inside of our soul, and find there a hidden treasure and a flower ready to bloom. We are all unique beings and the living witnesses of our lives, both actors and spectators of the human drama. To be serious is first and foremost to not take oneself seriously and to cherish the lightness of life. Equanimity in the face of challenges liberates a creative power and, because it inspires confidence, reassures those around us.

"Man is a rational animal who always loses his temper when called upon to act in accordance with the dictates of reason." (Oscar Wilde). To take risks is to feel alive and to overcome one's fears by making brave choices. Any virtuous decision enhances qualities and experience, and reduces stress and the fear of failure. It is neither appropriate to constrict oneself so as not to put oneself in danger, nor useful to want to protect others. The beauty of action resides in the uncertainty of the outcome. There is no obligation to succeed, only to try.

· 10 ·
FRIENDSHIP

From the earliest beginnings of sedentarization until the present, the social organization of the world has given structure to group living and developed the concept of friendship. This type of relationship has always existed, initially at family level, then between people of the same racial group and more recently of different groups which may have disparate origins. It has favored social relationships by establishing codes of conduct and principles for living. There is no meaning in the idea of friendship unless it is put to the test, since only action generates sentiments and a lasting affinity of the heart. It is different from love between two people, because no physical or psychic attraction is involved.

Confucius laid down the basic principles of living together, defining loyalty as one of the pillars of group life, which will not accept lies or deceit.

Loyalty is the foundation of enduring friendships. This essential quality is a commitment to another person, but can also come into play to defend a cause or an idea. It demands confidence, a knowledge of oneself and others, identity of thought and convergence of viewpoints. It is a bastion that protects the durability of relations.

Confucius laid down the basic principles of living together, defining loyalty as one of the pillars of group life, which will not accept lies or deceit. It is an invisible bond between people that exalts and magnifies relations, creating the conditions for closeness. This relational approach may apply to two or more people, whether or not of the same sex. It takes time and communication and has to pass through the filter of experience. Getting to know someone else is a privilege won through repeated meetings over time, in a virtuous framework favorable to the liberation of feelings and genuineness of commitment. Tests mobilize energies to be directed towards a common goal, uniting and transcending individuals.

Team sports, especially contact sports, create a special relationship between people of the same sex and sublimate fear, transforming it into shared energy that generates solidarity in the endeavor to reach a goal which is beyond the reach of team members individually. Group identity, compliance with common rules and community life bring people together and develop the conditions needed for individual and joint performance in pursuit of a shared ambition. Team spirit is established and supported by the leaders, the captain, the trainers or the manager. The latter, even if uninvolved in day-to-day decisions, represents the guardian of the temple who ensures the stability of the institution and its influence across the country or in the world. The sense of belonging and close relationship will outlast the sporting careers of the players and will live on in the hearts of all the members of the club. It will be sustained by an invisible bond, regular meetings and the duty to pass on the baton from one generation to the next. It is a collective culture that breathes meaning into the lives of every member of this "second family". A wink, a message or a meal nourishes friendship and strengthens this pure, generous sentiment.

The closeness bred of shared endeavor, difficult conditions or danger brings a natural hierarchy of relations into being. Moving in religious, philosophical or economic circles, we have the opportunity to meet other people with similar points of reference and to share common values and sometimes emotions. However, an ordinary, cocooned environment can never provide the same spirit of openness, the exaltation or the adrenalin that sport can bring.

Intimacy is the pinnacle of friendship. It is a virtuous demand founded on the quality and frequency of interactions, openness, give-and-take and acceptance of risk. To abandon oneself to another is the culmination of a deep, personal conquest.

Intimacy brings together a limited circle of people who share a given ideal, tried and tested, sincere, fraternal and devoid of any social power dynamic. It imposes courage, opens the doors to feelings and reveals the weaknesses and strengths of each person. It is providential for anyone seeking to understand human relations in the light of a chivalrous ideal. This implies an extreme sense of honor and a compelling urge to serve a greater cause, in the defense of the weaker and of justice. This code of conduct admits temporality, but also the immortality of the soul.

It is a spiritual path that demands nobility in action and the obligation to act as long as we live in the service of a cause that transcends us.

These three levels represent the hierarchy of friendship and open the door to an inner quest mingling the absolute, the beautiful, the being of Greek thought and the transcendental opening of the heart to God.

THE CIRCLES OF FRIENDSHIP

Our contemporary society of communication and the exponential growth of the virtual redefine the concept of friendship and abuse intimacy. Facebook was the first platform to rename data-processing links, changing the status of "contact" to that of "friend". This perversion has literally altered the attributes of friendship. The proliferation of messaging systems and connections of all classes and segments of the population with this virtual relationship has created social media icons, who have become "friends" and share their "stories" with you. This exhibitionism, bordering at times on immodesty, intensifies the superficiality of feelings and undermines their sincerity, creating models for uniform, condescending behavior.

The proliferation of "likes" becomes an accounting criterion for the efficacy of the message. Everything is measured, so that any virtual message of affection or friendship passes through the filter of logic, in order to potentialize the chances of success of this communication. The world of virtual "friendship" imposes a rhythm, a frequency of connection and updating of our digital identity if we are to stay "with it" in the social media sphere.

This unrestricted space sometimes releases fears and anxieties and can encourage discussions conducted without complexes or timidity, notably in adolescence, making it easier to take the first steps towards a "real" meeting. In contrast, these discussion platforms just as often deploy negative energies, violence or hate, especially from those who hide behind pseudonyms to pour out their stupidity or resentment.

In this way, the three pillars of friendship are mishandled by the speed of circulation of information, and also by the escalation of verbal attacks and violence. The younger generations, ceaselessly using these technologies, are not immune to cognitive fractures leading to indoctrination and the construction of a "dark education" which can culminate in terrorism or jihadism, but equally in other forms of conditioning based on perversion and alienation. The virtual world offers conditions favorable to isolation. The shifting points of reference and the longing to belong to an illusory community can generate tensions within the family and even lead to permanent breakups.

Friendship is a calm emotional condition, founded on benevolence, comradeship and sincerity of feelings. It is a lifebuoy that keeps our heads above water in difficult periods. It is genuine, resilient and unselfish, and has nothing in common with the illusory virtual world. It would be beneficial for the self-esteem of young people to redefine the concept of the social-media "friend" as a "contact", and avoid the temptation to live in the chimerical belief that the number of a person's Internet followers generates a personality, gives structure to thought and develops an ideal.

Communication, whether digital, verbal or non-verbal, is a tool used to express our thoughts.

Intimacy demands tried and tested self-knowledge, acceptance of our aspirations, a steadfast existential quest and an adaptable, generous attitude to others. It can be sublimated in the relationship between people who attain mutual harmony by confiding in each other, thereby nurturing each other's self-fulfillment.

Friendship is the unchanging foundation of a charitable, companionable humanity.

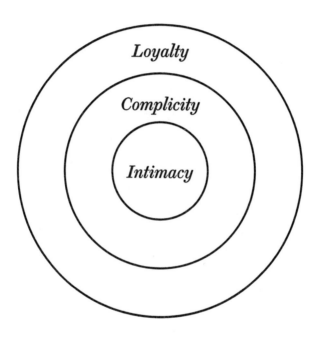

• THE CIRCLES OF FRIENDSHIP •

PART IV
TAKING CARE OF THE EARTH

THE CURRENT GLOBAL SITUATION AND OUTLOOK

The Earth supports the world and nourishes and regulates our organizational systems. The harmony of such organization brings us down to our humble human condition and makes us aware of the wonderful gift we are granted each day.

Everything seems so normal and natural that we rarely pause to wonder.

Life is a blessing. Although we have not been around long, we believe we have taken possession of the planet by our attempts to control it. We entertain the illusion that we are conducting this majestic symphony. Creation is perfect. The earth is connected to all the planets of the solar system. The moon, our satellite, dictates our seasons and our calendar. For thousands of years, the earth's clock has been in complete alignment with the heavenly organization of an expanding universe. It is this harmony that has enabled the evolution of mankind, from our earliest ancestors to the present day. The air we breathe, the water we drink, the food we eat and the sun which gives us warmth, and light to our days are the vital ingredients for our development, in keeping with this perpetual mechanism.

For more than ten thousand years, different civilizations have celebrated their art of living and their devotion to nature. Between myth and reality, we have been the witnesses of a slow evolution of the human condition, often via wars and conquests but also thanks to human resourcefulness and methodical organization. Some civilizations have disappeared. Plato, putting words in the mouth of Socrates in the 4th century B.C., makes mention of an Atlantean civilization, which dominated the world with arrogance and pride. A great power established on an island dominated Greece and Asia, and was home to a highly advanced culture and extraordinary fauna and flora. The warriors of Atlantis attempted to subjugate the Mediterranean but met with Greek resistance. Earthquakes and floods followed which, in a single day, swallowed up the island and its inhabitants. Legend, fiction or reality? The question remains. Be that as it may, we know that the earth, since its beginnings, has been subjected to disasters, continental drift and the extinction of species such as the dinosaurs.

Many of these changes have been the results of extraordinary events – the collisions of asteroids, volcanic eruptions causing fires that changed people's lives and the migratory routes of animals. The Mayan civilization also disappeared leaving behind it a belief system and a model of social life.

The Egyptians, Greeks and Romans created a meticulously ordered system of rules for living that are partly still in effect today.

The 20th century saw exponential population growth, the development of international relations, the Universal Declaration of Human Rights adopted by the UN in 1948, space exploration and an improvement in standards of living. We have been through wars and dark times, before experiencing decades of progress.

The first whistle-blowers on the state of the planet, in the second half of the 20th century, were not heard. It is always difficult to be right too early. And yet, we have seen an astonishing loss of biodiversity in the world. Several studies define the current situation as the sixth major extinction on earth. In the space of a hundred years, we have gone from a balanced habitat to state of major imbalance. The demographic explosion has been very quick. Human needs have increased, with a habitual diet much richer in protein and particularly meat, which has led to a greater need for agricultural land, both for livestock grazing and the growing of animal feed. This has caused intensified deforestation, particularly in Brazil, one of the leading producers of soybeans in the world. We also consume more and more fish, and overfishing is threatening many marine species with extinction.

These problems affect all continents. Africa has been strongly impacted by global warming, overpopulation, drinking water shortages and malnutrition. The continent is a ticking time bomb which will eventually explode if population growth continues at the current rate. In Asia, the state of pastures and prairies is not reassuring and many endemic species are under threat. In North and South America, a land of pioneers, landscapes and forests have undergone changes that are of grave concern. The latter continent is home to natural resources which must be protected. The forests in the Amazon are the lungs of the planet, their disgraceful exploitation for the sole profit of a minority must be stopped.

The nations of the Pacific are not spared either. Australia, in particular, is paying the price of the amateurism of its leaders and the absence of a proper plan to protect its natural wealth, notably its forests. The fires in early 2020 were a true environmental catastrophe. More than six million hectares went up in smoke, and with them many living species and millions of animals. This is equivalent to an area greater than countries like Belgium or Costa Rica. Australia's carbon footprint is disastrous. Each hectare of forest destroyed ceases to produce oxygen or store carbon. In contrast, the fires released into the atmosphere the equivalent of one hundred and eighty million tons of carbon, or six hundred million tons of CO_2. According to the Copernicus observation program, this is equal to the annual carbon emissions of the one hundred and sixteen least polluting nations of the world. These sudden emissions will add to global warming which, in turn, will aggravate rain scarcity and forest fires. It will take decades for these devastated areas to be restored.

In Europe also, in spite of effective population management, the militant activism of a number of associations and continuously growing environmental awareness, biodiversity is decreasing. In France, this is due largely to intensive agriculture and the overuse of chemicals, which deplete soils and increase their salinity. Used to excess, chemical fertilizers such as potash and phosphorus contribute to increased phytotoxicity and loss of soil fertility. In Germany, arthropod biomass has fallen by thirty to fifty percent, depending on the area. Waterways, streams and rivers are also impacted by human activities, factory waste and the widespread use of glyphosate.

In France, the loss of biodiversity is due largely to intensive agriculture and the overuse of chemicals, which deplete soils and increase their salinity.

Tests on human hair have demonstrated that these substances travel up the food chain and end up being ingested by humans and animals. Many pulmonary and vascular diseases, and diseases of the joints and brain, are directly or indirectly linked to the quality of the air we breathe, the water we drink and the foods we eat. The salinization and warming of the seas cause climate disruption and increase the frequency of the hurricanes, storms or cyclones that devastate our countries and our towns, kill thousands of people and cost nations and insurance companies a fortune.

Pollution, as surprising as this may seem, can also come from the intensification of magnetic fields. Human beings and plants are an assembly of cells connected by desmosomes. The flow of electrons conditions the harmonious use of cellular membranes–yet electromagnetic waves disrupt this flow.

For more than a hundred years, we have been witnessing the electrification of the earth, for which humans are unprepared. They would have to adjust and become stronger on a physiological level, and even more so have strength in their state of awareness, in order to resist this invisible pollution. In the 19th century, electromagnetic pollution did not yet exist. Since then we have been successively subjected to the effects of radio waves, radars, Wi-Fi, Bluetooth, 3G, 4G and now 5G. Consequently, mankind is constantly under attack. It is therefore highly unadvisable, for people's physical and mental balance, to live permanently near these fields.

Satellite launches have become commonplace, as a result of the development of telephone networks and their use for private, professional or military purposes.

Several thousand satellites currently orbit the earth, and their life span varies between ten and twenty years. Some, at the end of their period of usefulness, are destroyed by the atmosphere, while others end up in a zone called the celestial equator. Several thousand more are in the process of being launched and will surround the earth in all layers of the atmosphere.

Expanding electromagnetic fields can adversely affect people. Some fall ill, the rest of the population adjusts and carries on.

For several decades, progress has made possible an unprecedented improvement in quality of life and the circulation of goods, services and information. But man seems to have forgotten he is not just an earthly being but also a cosmic one. We are connected to nature and to the universe. A Van Allen belt's role is to capture the cosmic rays emanating from the Sun, the Moon and the other planets of the solar system, in order to distribute them to all living beings and thereby enable life on earth. Today's increasingly urban society is losing this invisible connection to nature and the universe. The situation is troubling, because electromagnetic pollution is currently neither supervised nor subject to legislation.

Interferences with planet Earth require the expertise of independent specialists, whose goal would be to preserve the delicate balance of our ecosystems and give human beings the time to adapt to changes with mindful awareness, while safeguarding the quality of life of future generations. The pollution of water, soils and the atmosphere is a multifaceted issue that is too important not to be dealt with by independent worldwide organizations dedicated to protecting our planet.

Far too many extraordinary events have occurred over the last ten years for us to believe in coincidence. The proliferation, frequency and violence of tornadoes and hurricanes, megafires (California, Australia), the global Covid-19 pandemic, disasters caused by drought not only in hot countries but also in Europe, not to mention generalized climate disturbance, are like alarm bells from nature, weakened by human activities. She is reasserting her rights, and, in a way, avenging so many onslaughts.

We are at a fork in the road – we must rethink our way of life and our role in the universe, based on an understanding of our connection with the planets and with the living world. It is high time to take action, opening our hearts and supporting sustainable, fair solutions that are compatible with the issues of today and tomorrow, for the advent of a better, caring, respectful and resilient world.

· 12 ·
URBAN LIVING IN THE COUNTRY

In the course of the 20th century, life in the industrialized countries shifted from a rural, agricultural mode to an urban one. The megalopolis is a recent phenomenon, whose appearance has significantly disrupted the rhythm of life for many people. More than 70 percent of us live in cities and towns. However, we need to distinguish large conurbations from those with under a hundred thousand inhabitants: the former are endowed with "green lungs", while the latter provide access to nature, fields and woods.

We all live on the same planet, but at varying rhythms and with different degrees of sensitivity to the environment and the cosmos. Street lighting and pollution tend to disconnect the citizen from the duality of Earth and Heaven. To look far away, glimpse the horizon, notice the direction of the wind in the daytime or clearly see the stars after nightfall and marvel at the celestial map of the night sky – access to these experiences is difficult for city dwellers. The absence of the vertical dimension sometimes engenders a feeling of anxiety, distress and sadness.

The daily round in big cities is often monotonous, governed by the repetitive tripartite subway-work-sleep routine. It standardizes habits, timed to the minute. Yet public and private services can provide an interesting, even vibrant life, offering far more potential activities than the urbanite could ever engage in.

The automobile remains the most used mode of transport. Traffic has reached saturation point, pollution is increasing and population growth will not improve the situation. Carbon dioxide is the primary source of pollution on the planet and contributes to global warming.

The solution will come from the younger generations, who choose public transport, car sharing and vehicle rental. Some initiatives, such as the development of cycle lanes, alternating traffic flow and short-range electric vehicles are interesting possible solutions to improving everyday life. New technologies involving reduced consumption of fossil fuels are an element in the energy transition and contribute to reducing nuisance levels.

Village life, especially in European countries, expresses different needs for each age group. Children benefit from the enjoyment of open-air life, the proximity of their schools and the security of their surroundings. The tranquility and connection with nature develop serenity, happiness and creativity. Teenagers take the bus every morning to go to their junior or high school in the neighboring town and return in the evening after a busy day of study. They inhabit the best of both worlds, and in spite of the tiring commute, they find themselves back in their familiar surroundings every night. Adults mostly obey a similar routine. Those who stay put enjoy comfortable living conditions and a state of balance that favor personal fulfillment.

Some contribute to the food chain, working in the agricultural sector. We are witnessing the development of a circular economy and the rediscovery of local produce. This familiarizes us anew with the cycle of the seasons and a healthy, varied diet. The farming world has changed considerably, but in every region, it remains bound up with local production potential and customs.

Country life could be encouraged by the authorities because, founded as it is on a different equilibrium, it provides a pleasanter, more harmonious mode of existence. In developing countries, most people live in less densely populated areas and are settled in villages or tribes. These populations are basically sedentarized, and live in an ancestral system dedicated to the production of basic necessities. The family dimension constitutes a force for cohesion and integration, conserving tried and tested life skills. The quality and amount of the harvest determine the conditions of the year to come: variations in the annual cycle, however, can quickly weaken this mode of organization in the event of climatic disruption, though this is more often the consequence of a drop in prices on the commodity market.

Among the world population, two billion people consume too much and five billion use the resources of the planet sparingly and with moderation.

The human spirit and the arrival of global communications, taken together, create expectations and needs in people who dream of a different world and a more reassuring future. The integration of these people who are seeking their place in the modern world will only be possible if their projects are included in the process of change and the vision of a better world.

Developing countries, in particular, need to create education systems giving every girl and boy equal access to schooling in order to eliminate illiteracy. Children's horizons must not be confined to those of their parents. They must have the opportunity, as children in rich countries do, to develop their creativity and garner knowledge acquired from elsewhere in the course of their education. This is the best way for emerging countries to remain stable and keep the brain drain and emigration in check, by creating wealth and economic development in their home territories. Better-balanced living conditions with prospects for growth and patriotic pride provide a favorable framework for personal and community development. To mirror this, the industrialized world needs to take inspiration from the wisdom and know-how of these groups and their deep historic and cultural roots.

The connection with the natural world and the cycle of seasonal tasks root human beings in an existence which is sometimes laborious and monotonous, but is less stressful than modern life.

Sowing, germination, flowering and picking are the eternal pattern that gives form to social life. The beauty of the world, the perfection of creation and the preservation of biodiversity rest in the hands of these people who, in all humility, represent bastions against the greed of some multinational organizations spawned by the ultraliberal system.

A third of the world's population lives in rich countries, admittedly in conditions of increasing inequality, but nevertheless enjoying a life of incomparably greater comfort than that of the other two thirds, who live simply and frugally. For the first group, time flies and the overabundance of goods and services develops new needs, sometimes out of reach. This generates frustration, anger and rebellion.

The digital world offers limitless virtual access to much of the learning accumulated over the last five thousand years, creating the conditions for a feeling of freedom and infinite knowledge. But there is another side to the coin: the alienation that comes with dependence on the system and the disappearance of the concept of private life. A world running at different speeds in a state of permanent change does not ensure that everyone can choose their future.

The complexity of the issues at stake, the exponential proliferation of discoveries and runaway birth rates in poor countries show the urgent need for a social reorganization corresponding to the priorities of each nation as well as the limited resources of our planet in order to ensure sustainable development. Economic competition and the race for world leadership between Europe, the United States and China are a threat to the planet. The need to build a benevolent model based on consensus between nations has become crucial.

There is no single perfect mode of organization that will provide health, happiness, wealth and freedom.

The people themselves must be determined to organize their systems while preserving the biosphere and natural equilibria. Urban living in the country is not such an important challenge as integrating a model of urbanized country life–bringing the country into harmony with the city, as it were. Education in developing countries will give everyone access to data, logistical and trade systems which will conserve the traditional models and achieve a better balance between rural and urban modes of living.

The men and women of the 21st century face a huge challenge. Living peacefully, free and happy in a connected world, is within the grasp of all. But it is an aspiration which can only be fulfilled by first preserving the hopes and stability of those whose care it is to feed the others. To meet the challenge of population growth, a good quality, balanced diet is an unconditional prerequisite. Our Earth that sustains us is the vital store that will make it possible to feed a growing world population. We must do two things: one is to take care of soil fertility and the purity of watercourses, and the other is to reduce the use of synthetic substances–herbicides, fungicides and insecticides. In addition, the use of phosphate fertilizers should be limited so as not to intensify the salinization of soils and subsoils. Monoculture will give way to polyculture wherever feasible. Bees, which pollinate flowers and play a key role in natural harmony, must be preserved.

The food policies of rich countries will need to change direction and favor seasonal foods, which are healthier and contain less protein.

Reviving local agriculture will ensure the quality and availability of regional products while respecting biodiversity, as in the case, for example, of traditional cereal crop varieties of high nutritive value. The fight against the standardization of seeds is wholly justified. It is vital to maintain and strengthen the production of local varieties, which are better adapted to the climate and soils of each region.

Reviving local agriculture will ensure the quality and availability of regional products while respecting biodiversity.

Smallholders have a decisive role to play in farming worldwide. They will be more powerful and better organized if they join forces and offer commonsense development plans. The farmer's vocation is not limited to the practice of agriculture: he also looks after the landscape and the environment. It is important to instill the desire to work in this sector in the younger generations, with guarantees relating to income and stronger contract conditions. The trade in coffee, tea and cocoa, on the global level, encourages fair partnerships with the producers. The creation of circular economies presents many advantages in terms of shorter distribution chains, better carbon balance and, last but not least, fresh, healthy produce, rich in vitamins and minerals that contribute to improvements in well-being.

All over the world, success in the face of these issues depends on a better equilibrium between town and country. Large cities could establish green cultivation zones in each neighborhood.

Agricultural policies will be the key to living better together in future. We must invent new social models ensuring a peaceful, balanced and harmonious life in a sustainable world where the priorities of each person are respected.

· 13 ·
FROM ORGANIC TO BIODYNAMIC

From food to health, there is only a small step to better understanding what is on the line when it comes to agriculture and the preservation of the ecosystems of our planet. Feeding seven and a half billion humans is an enormous challenge if we consider the complexity of current food product organization. The carbon footprint related to the exchange of goods is too high, and continues to grow as the needs of people with access to a market economy increase.

Extreme trade liberalization and the globalization of the economy have created ruthless competition around all food products, particularly fresh produce such as milk, butter, fish, meat, fruits and vegetables. There is a huge range of choice, increasingly divorced from the seasons so as to guarantee constant supply. This system is the norm in all Western countries.

The most striking example is that of the tomato, produced mainly in the Netherlands and in Spain. Our Dutch neighbors grow tomatoes in gigantic greenhouses and we can regard such fruits as having the color and shape of tomatoes but not their flavor. Their nutritional value is very low and residual traces of pesticides high. In Spain, granted, there is more sunshine, but the production model is identical, requiring permanent irrigation which drains the groundwater in Andalusia and Extremadura. We could also cite salad, zucchinis and many other vegetables. This product-oriented model utilizes large amounts of fertilizers, energy and various kinds of pesticides. The majority of children do not know what a tomato tastes like, simply because it no longer tastes of anything. In normal conditions, in the northern hemisphere, this seasonal fruit offers us its flavor from June to September. Mediterranean countries, France, Spain, Italy, Greece, Turkey and many others, have created many tomato-based recipes that combine them with eggs, olives, cheeses, vegetables and so on. There are numerous varieties – preserved by agricultural conservationists – which our fellow citizens never have the pleasure of sampling. It is important to fight against the standardization of taste and offer. The cluster tomato mainly sold in our countries is the antithesis of good taste and an insult to Mediterranean cooking. Its only redeeming feature is its price and the duration of its shelf life.

Changing the system requires a willingness to relocalize the production of fruits and vegetables and establish an ethical economic model that strengthens local partnerships with businesses of various sizes who, while respecting organic production rules, would provide seasonal produce all year round, harvested at the right degree of ripeness, and offer a far wider and far better quality range of choice. The carbon footprint would be lower, as would water consumption, and the taste immeasurably superior. Admittedly, the price would be higher but the pleasure incomparable, and such produce would keep far longer. The consumer would benefit, and nutritional quality and flavor would be reinstated as main priorities.

The transition to organic farming is undeniably challenging, since it requires that farms implement major changes in terms of staffing, planting density, supervision and picking. The economic model is different, but the investments made will prove judicious in the long term in the context of a policy of contractualization with increasingly dynamic retailers. The first two years of converting to organic or biodynamic require that methods be changed, teams be trained and equipment replaced. In France, conversion exists as a legal status and this guarantees fair remuneration to growers. The use of organic fertilizers instead of chemical ones and the discontinuation of phytosanitary products create a new equilibrium, which may be less production-oriented but is more sustainable, since it is friendly towards the surrounding biodiversity, the watercourses, the natural taste of fruits and vegetables, and their nutritional value. It also respects the health of consumers. Organic farming is life, health and a return to nature. This model which, let us not forget, was the norm for more than five thousand years, has suffered from the development of a product-oriented and highly mechanized form of agriculture put in place forty years ago initially in response to the need to feed a population exhausted by the post-war years. Later, once this goal had been achieved, it obeyed only the requirements of the market and the aggressive demands of purchasing platforms.

The use of organic fertilizers instead of chemical ones and the discontinuation of phytosanitary products create a new equilibrium, which may be less production-oriented but is more sustainable, since it is friendly towards the surrounding biodiversity, the watercourses, the natural taste of fruits and vegetables, and their nutritional value.

It is time to go back to basics, to guarantee our fellow citizens a diet rich in vitamins, minerals and trace elements, free of residual pesticides and preservatives. We must urgently establish priorities for our governments, without waiting for agricultural policies to supersede people's needs. The education of our children at school, with the spread of organic school kitchens in some regions, is a step in the right direction. Once they discover the taste of food and its seasonality, pupils begin to influence the purchases of their parents. Organic farming today is an appropriate and proven system that can guarantee quantity–while it cannot yet supply all markets, this could happen before long if consumers support it. It will take a few years to change systems in wealthy countries.

We must have faith in the power of group purchasing organizations and major global distribution groups to change, because they have already understood where the future lies. Major investments in infrastructure must be made, and grants put in place for young farmers setting up. This new qualitative and ethical model will guarantee better health for people, and therefore de facto reduce medical costs.

To eat less, but well–sedentary man has lost the ancestral nutritional balance that was based on the energy needs of a farming population connected to nature. The day would begin with a hearty breakfast, followed by a light lunch and a frugal dinner. This distribution of calorie rations was adjusted to the needs of the body, to the rhythm of the day and time for rest. The body burns fat from midnight to midday and stores it from midday to midnight. Any excessive intake of calories in the afternoon or evening will be stored and turned into fat, especially in subjects leading a sedentary lifestyle. Continued overindulgence in the evenings disturbs sleep and therefore rest.

Common sense shows us the way, if we are prepared to listen to the body, pay attention to balance and respect our biological clocks. Following these principles does not imply they can never be transgressed and life not enjoyed on appropriate occasions when good cheer and company beckon. The goal is not to lead a monastic life, but to alternate periods of plenty with more frugal ones. This is what being epicurean means–to meet genuine and natural needs. To his disciples,

Epicurus passed on strength of character, and a conceptual balance situated between asceticism and hedonism. This doctrine is a popular materialist philosophy based on sensation, truth and friendship.

Consumer society has turned people's priorities upside down, and interfered with their areas of interest. Food has no spiritual or philosophical significance. It must meet expectations and calorie needs. New gastronomy has unchained itself from the fundamentals of Escoffier, the precursor and father of modern French cuisine. Top starred chefs such as Alain Ducasse, Anne-Sophie Pic, Pierre Gagnaire, Hélène Darroze, Guy Savoy, Gilles Goujon and many others are focusing once more on seasonal products, often organic, but also offering amazing experiences using vegetables. These opinion leaders have a considerable impact on our behavior, since in cooking as in wine-growing, verticality and balance, subtlety and complexity awaken our senses and our taste buds.

The same goes for agriculture. For a long time, organic and biodynamic farming were the prerogative of a closed circle of practitioners leading a self-sufficient life. These pioneers blazed a trail by demonstrating the sustainability of these methods which are free of synthetic products. Subsequently, the spread of organic products, in compliance with strict labels such as the AB mark in France, Ecocert in Europe and USDA Organic in the United States, led to increased demand and the provision of regular supply, accessible to all and of high quality. Wine production has followed this movement. New labels go even further, to accommodate the needs of those who suffer from food intolerances, for example sulfites in wine, but also to align with the rising vegan wave. Elsewhere, in the Cévennes valley, many wine growers and farmers, under the umbrella of the Bee-Friendly label, are working to protect bees and pollinators. They use no products that might harm these insects that are so precious for the harmony of our ecosystems.

France, Germany, Spain, Italy and Switzerland are all wine producing countries that are standards of reference around the world. They have spent time and effort on the development of wines of great delicacy, that reveal "the taste of somewhere". The qualities of the local growing environment are brought out when the soil is alive – grapes of the terroir pick up the imprint of their biotope thanks to the wind, the sun and the rain and, through the alchemy of fermentation, release these traces of their origin into the wine.

Going from simple know-how to farming and wine-growing know-how requires vision, courage and the desire to share. These new and experimental methods have paved the way for a rethink on sustainable, productive farming. Tomorrow's model, integrated and local, will be organic or will not exist at all, because people, especially urban populations, will be demanding it. Astute farmers and wine growers have demonstrated with brio that it is possible to develop organic and even biodynamic farming on large acreages, in accordance with the vision of Rudolf Steiner who, in his reference work, The Agricultural Course, sings the praises of farming entities. This successful experiment represents hope that these growing techniques may become mainstream in the decades to come.

New architectural projects will include spaces to grow things in the heart of cities. In this way, anybody, on their terrace or on their balcony, will be able to grow a few chosen fruits or vegetables and express their solidarity with those who make their living from the land.

Biodynamics practiced for a hundred years in Europe and now all over the world, proposed a new integrative model based on biodiversity and the interaction between the forces of the cosmos and the earth. This transcendental dimension opens our eyes to the beauty of the universe and an understanding of the subtle equilibria found in nature. Our system is dependent upon the light and energy of the sun. This tenuous balance is subject to the variability of temperatures and reliant upon the protection of our environment. Nature fixes the rules, and we are obliged to adapt to them.

Life belongs not to the earth but to the sun. If a dark veil were to be placed above us, nothing would grow any more. Life forces come from the cosmos and enable roots to use the microorganisms in the soil to assist in the growth and nutrition of the plant. In contrast, herbicides destroy the microbial life in the ground, leading to a need for chemical fertilizers to compensate.

However, these fertilizers are like salts that increase the plant's need for water and weaken it, making it vulnerable to sicknesses, which, in turn, are treated with systemic synthetic products, brutally effective because they get into the sap. Yet this is precisely how they disrupt the plant's functioning, because it is through the sap that it picks up weather signals.

Wines made using conventional production methods can be technically well engineered and give pleasure to the consumer, but they cannot reveal the unique taste of the terroir that gave birth to them, especially if synthetic substances such as herbicides, insecticides and fungicides are regularly used. Regarding moderate use of sulfur and copper in wines, the debate is nonsensical because both are natural elements in the living world, like oxygen or hydrogen. Garlic, onion and rocket also naturally contain sulfur.

We therefore make a distinction between wines belonging to nowhere and terroir wines. In order to identify them, all that is required is to open a bottle, taste the wine, and come back a week later to taste it again. The wine that received life energy will have survived, the technically manipulated one will not.

The sun is the main power supply for plants. Its energy reaches us on frequencies and wavelengths that are currently interfered with by millions of radio waves in all layers of the atmosphere. The earth receives less life energy. It is suffering and beginning to rebel. The magnetic north pole is now eight hundred kilometers away from where it should be.

Biodynamics goes further than organic farming in that it practices the dynamization of water according to the vortex principal, and the spraying of homeopathic doses of plant-based blends (nettle, chamomile, yarrow), or concoctions designated by numbers, like 501, 502 or 503.

The earth, in order to regenerate and renew itself, could reverse its magnetic poles, just as it has done already several times since its creation. This would trigger extraordinary events, the impact of which on our civilization is unknown, but with consequences that could be dire for some of humanity.

The concept of biodynamics created by Rudolf Steiner nurtures the health of the soil and plants, which follows the rhythm of heavenly bodies and the moon. It prohibits all use of chemical products. It is certified by referent organizations such as Demeter or Biodivin, whose reliability and exacting requirements are a safeguard for the consumer. Biodynamics goes further than organic farming in that it practices the dynamization of water according to the vortex principal, and the spraying of homeopathic doses of plant-based blends (nettle, chamomile, yarrow), or concoctions designated by numbers, like 501, 502 or 503. Each one is linked to a planet, for example Mercury or Venus. All act as receivers for microbial life, the archetype of which is a planet.

This approach, which respects the soil (with the practice of polyculture) to protect biodiversity and the longevity of ecosystems, is also philosophical, in that it develops a more profound understanding of the living world.

· 14 ·
CLIMATE CHANGE, ECOLOGY AND THE ENERGY TRANSITION

Over the last twenty years, we have witnessed climate perturbations which seem to result principally from human activity, especially by greenhouse gases. The increase in the use of fossil fuels and natural gas is a consequence of the combined needs of industry and transport and the rise in the number of motorists, but also the growing needs of agriculture and domestic consumption.

The three largest polluters in the world are China, the United States and Europe. COP21 and the Paris Agreement of 2015 set an upper limit of 1.5°C to the increase in global average temperature by 2050, and the goal of achieving a balance between greenhouse gases emitted by human activity and those absorbed by carbon sinks. The rich countries also undertook to pay a minimum of one hundred billion dollars per year from 2020 on. This agreement was signed by 195 countries before the withdrawal of the United States, by which this important step forward was rendered obsolete, casting doubt on the strategy that had been ratified, despite the plan for the reforestation of three hundred and fifty million hectares of land drawn up at the COP23 in Bonn. President Joe Biden's confirmation of the return of the USA offers a ray of hope.

Our planet Earth has gone through a series of different climatic periods related to continental drift and different periods of glaciation. Prehistoric times were especially difficult. About seventy million years ago, it was so cold that certain bodies of water were frozen solid and sea levels dropped by some one hundred meters. The population of the Earth at that time was of the order of fifteen to twenty thousand people. During the Holocene, temperatures returned to a level still cool, but

———————

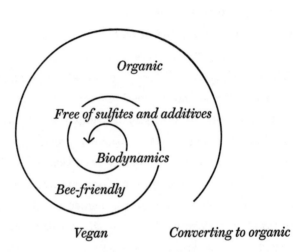

Organic

Free of sulfites and additives

Biodynamics

Bee-friendly

Vegan   Converting to organic

• THE LIVING AGRICULTURE SPIRAL •

———————

favorable to human development. Humankind discovered agriculture, sedentarization and the stability of tribal life. It was the start of a new era, when water management techniques adapted to the seasons were used to safeguard harvests, making it possible to feed whole groups with rice, corn and other early cereal varieties.

At the beginning of the 20th century, global population was about one and half billion, and life expectancy was much shorter than it is today. The exponentially rising growth rate of the human race, the development of trade, the increasing consumption of fossil fuels and longer life expectancy have created the conditions for an ecological catastrophe. Today, we have reached a figure of about seven billion people, and the ten to twelve billion that planners predict before the end of the century threaten the total collapse of our system.

At present, all indicators are on red alert: the seas are polluted, with rising acidity levels; deforestation is on the increase; the appalling air quality in our cities is causing chronic lung diseases. Greenhouse gases are heating the planet, melting the ice caps and raising sea levels. Biodiversity is waning: the disappearance of plants and of 60 percent of wildlife species in forty years is throwing the living world into disarray.

The facts are alarming, and we are unable to put forward proposals for long-term change which could first put a cap on rising temperatures and then restore biodiversity. This requires radical changes which will call upon all the resources of human ingenuity and especially the wisdom of governments and people. In the last few years, we have witnessed an upsurge in natural disasters such as hurricanes, cyclones, droughts and consequent forest fires. In the last two years, the large number of fires has had terrible effects on the natural habitat and global warming.

We need to find solutions to unprecedented migration problems, as people flee not only from destitution, malnutrition and climatic disruption, but also from totalitarian regimes at their last gasp.

Our capacity to forget these major crises and fail to learn from them is mind-blowing. Climate skeptics continue to support the existing system. The reaction of Planet Earth to these ongoing attacks will not be linear. Far-reaching

Our capacity to forget these major crises and fail to learn from them is mind-blowing.

changes cannot be ruled out, such as the disappearance of the Gulf Stream, the warm current that originates in the Gulf of Mexico and plays a role in regulating the climate of Europe. Thawing of the Arctic permafrost could cause a resurgence of viruses and bacteria contained in plants, animals or remains of human corpses preserved in the ice.

As regards demography, it is in Africa that the greatest population explosion is feared. United Nations experts predict that the population will increase from 1.3 billion in 2020 to 2.5 billion in 2050. This would pose considerable problems in the areas of health, water and nutrition, as well as immense difficulties of access to the labor market and regulation of the economy.

The population of countries in other parts of the world will also continue to grow, but at lower rates.

Many experts hold that world population must not exceed eight billion, in order to avoid exhausting the natural resources of the planet and to be able to set out a regulation plan that would respect human rights and individual liberty. This is an enormous challenge which can only be met by collective action and shared effort, involving the richest and most polluting countries in particular.

The solutions found in the nineteen nineties which halted the destruction of the ozone layer and the associated UV radiation offer a ray of hope for the human race. Admittedly, such corrective actions as the prohibition of CFCs in aerosols did not entail much inconvenience for the consumer.

We now need to take action on the big questions of the 21st century: population growth, biodiversity, soil fertility, reforestation, clean oceans, sustainable fishing, a diet less rich in protein, alternative energies, the circular economy, air quality, public transport and organic farming.

Population growth is a highly complex problem, because it is uneven around the world and depends on subtle factors. It was encouraged after the war to repopulate ravaged countries, especially in Europe, and to boost economic growth. Procreation is the natural result of living as a couple and a desire that is often crucial to its success. Population balance with its "inputs and outputs" was satisfactory from the Middle Ages until the 1980s, because it was regulated by high infant mortality rates, epidemics, wars, famines, food shortages and floods.

Population growth has increased, with very high rates in the last fifty years, to the great satisfaction of dominant countries, because markets have been sustained and economic development required cheap labor originating from developing countries. In the latter, precarious standards of living and insecurity made any kind of planning extremely difficult. Inadequate educational systems and strong religious influence promoted reproduction; recourse to contraception was and sometimes still is limited; and the right to abortion in case of unwanted pregnancy is not recognized everywhere, and also poses ethical problems that remain unresolved.

Emancipation of women, generalized access to the job market and the economic crisis have lowered birthrates in Europe and the USA. France and Ireland have succeeded in maintaining a rate greater than two children per family, thanks to financial policies offering incentives. In other major countries, such as Germany, but also China, an aging population and a falling fertility rate are very soon going to cause economic problems. In contrast, African countries and, to a lesser degree, those of Latin America, continue to display growth, destroying any hope of stabilizing world population in the short term.

For the equilibrium of our planet, it is essential to control the number of inhabitants so that everyone can have access to education, a good-quality diet and professional and family prospects corresponding to their ideals. This challenge is a priority. Our resources are not infinite and our present-day consumerist model must be transformed: the carbon footprint of the rich countries must be considerably reduced and birthrates in Africa must be controlled by creating awareness of the issues at stake among society at large, but also by education for girls and equal rights.

Africa possesses undreamed-of resources, incredible resilience and exceptional vitality. It is the duty of the West to help the continent to work out democratic and economic programs that are constructive and equitable. Improving living conditions could moderate the growth curve and create the conditions for development which would stabilize African unity and indirectly enable our planet to give all its inhabitants the fundamentals of access to good-quality water and air, education and the hope of a better life.

Biodiversity is subjected to ongoing onslaughts caused by human activity: overfishing, overexploitation of resources, excessive use of chemical products, proliferation of genetically modified organisms and destruction of pollinators.

After the end of the First World War, armament factories were converted to produce chemical fertilizers, the use of which immediately improved agricultural yields. After ten years of intensive use of this chemical input, the resulting salinization had degraded the fertility of the soil and subsoil. The generalized use of the synthetic products that made their appearance in the sixties has turned out to be a disservice to the farming world, creating a degraded system, harmful to the biotope and users alike.

This endless race for productivity to withstand the competition of the markets and match world foodstuff prices is completely senseless and leads to intensive farming, in thrall to the agrochemical industry. These days, the price of cereals, soya and sugar are defined like oil prices.

What contempt for those who spend their days caring for the soil, showing consideration for biodiversity and the landscape!

It will be advantageous to go back to sowing local seeds, which are better adapted to their area, and to retail these products locally, which is a more equitable system with a smaller carbon footprint. Reviving a more ethical, organic agriculture will be friendly to soils and subsoils and produce balanced yields with higher nutritional quality and better keeping properties.

The Indian region of Sikkim is an encouraging example. All farming there is organic, because the State has prohibited the use of any artificial inputs. This bold political decision has generated a new qualitative model which respects the environment, raises the status of the farmers and is providential for the consumer. Observation has established that yields have increased and people's health has improved. Bringing agriculture back into harmony with local conditions is a vital step and will form one of the pillars of the ecological transition.

Soil fertility is directly linked to microbial life. This underground habitat is a complicated mechanism of interconnections which constitutes the breeding ground of our lives. Humidity levels are crucially important here. They will be maintained by mechanical aeration of the soil, but also by putting an end to the toxicity to plant life that has resulted from the large-scale use of chemicals.

Water is a vital resource which, in some regions of the world that suffer from dry climates, is essential for population stability. Collecting rainwater and optimizing its use are priorities. The development of hillside catchment reservoirs, rainwater collection systems in towns and dams that respect the needs of the local population could be encouraged and become widespread in dry areas. The sinking of wells must be controlled in order to enable water tables to be replenished and avoid jeopardizing subsequent irrigation.

The circular economy is a conceptual model of the economic cycle from basic needs to consumption in a sustainable virtuous circle that incorporates recycling, waste management and moderation in the use of packaging. This concept throws light on the waste and exhaustion of natural resources. It works on the principle of renewable energy and reducing single use. It is a controversial model in the present-day world, which is founded on growth, but this new direction is not incompatible with a consumer society. It puts forward solutions that use less energy and pay greater respect to the living world. This anthropological leap forward will be able to reap considerable benefits from certain technologies, in particular the 3D printer, which will significantly diminish raw material needs and the carbon footprint of products manufactured.

The reforestation plan determined at the COP23 in Bonn will help to improve carbon capture. In addition to this ambitious program, every human being should symbolically plant a tree each year as a contribution to reforestation, to renew their bond with nature and create awareness of the living world.

The oceans have become the garbage can of the modern world, especially the dump for single-use plastics. The sea suffers as much as the land from the excesses of our civilization. Fishing must respect the different species and new quotas need to be established to ensure their revival. Today, overfishing threatens some species, such as wild salmon, grouper, bluefin tuna and cod, and even more serious is the WWF assessment that, at present rates, there will be no fish left in the oceans by 2048. So what are we waiting for to establish an international system of regulation to limit tonnage, while also working towards a healthy diet containing less protein?

The human animal is omnivorous, and has developed its cerebral faculties from a high-protein diet. But our calorie intake is completely out of proportion to that of prehistoric times, as are our energy expenditure and life expectancy. Most people do not use the calories they have consumed in the form of regular physical activity. Our diet has improved considerably, but in statistical terms, our consumption of proteins, especially meat, has soared.

The consumption of beef, due to its attractive flavor, its availability and its modest price, has escalated to the point of excess causing health problems. Meat consumption has risen from sixty to three hundred million tons in the last fifty years. Cattle rearing is the source of 15 percent of our greenhouse gas emissions–as much as global transport. Pork and chicken consume much less carbon than beef.

It is necessary for our health and good for the planet to improve the ratio between proteins of animal and vegetable origin in our diet. Reducing our daily intake of protein and calories is a responsible and

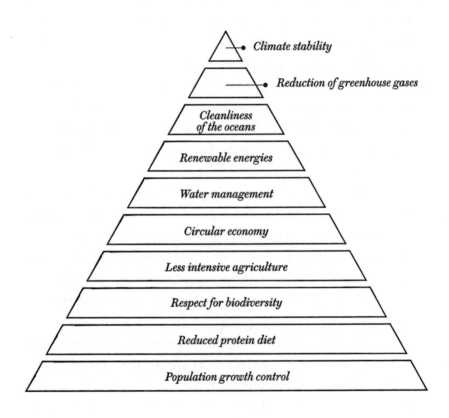

Climate stability

Reduction of greenhouse gases

Cleanliness
of the oceans

Renewable energies

Water management

Circular economy

Less intensive agriculture

Respect for biodiversity

Reduced protein diet

Population growth control

• ENVIRONMENTAL AND ENERGY TRANSITION PYRAMID •

ethical course of action. The creativity of culinary advisors and the recommendations of nutritionists offer painless alternatives.

The human revolution begins on our plates. Meat consumption per head in Europe and the United States is about 80 kilograms per year, which is double the global average. If nothing is done, forecasts show that this consumption of meat products will continue to grow. A global plan will have to be enacted to reduce this rate of consumption, especially in the rich countries where health problems and obesity have reached alarming proportions. The objective of a 30 percent reduction to two hundred million tons would be ambitious but attainable, because today numerous appetizing sources of protein-rich food are known. Furthermore, the water input to produce a kilogram of meat is fifteen thousand liters: fifty times more than for a kilogram of potatoes.

Eating is a socially responsible activity. The most fundamental act of solidarity is to make it possible for others to feed themselves properly with due consideration for diversity, customs and traditions. Eating better is a step towards reducing greenhouse gas emissions, making agriculture less intensive, bringing back local production, drastically reducing oilseed needs and halting deforestation, which will have a positive feedback effect on our ecosystems, air quality, carbon storage and decelerated global warming.

The issue of domestic heating and electricity use, representing 30 percent of carbon consumption, has been grasped by governments and the building industry, which propose materials offering better insulation and a range of solutions such as geothermal and photovoltaic heating and renewable resources such as wind turbines. The energy transition plan must be encouraged and established on an equitable basis around the world so as to limit the growth of needs and escape from oil dependence. Natural resources, especially those derived from the sun and wind energy, are a sector to be prioritized, because they are inexhaustible, even if the conversion of wind energy into electricity itself requires considerable energy input.

We have moved from a situation of abundance to the threat of shortage. The intensive use of non-renewable resources, especially fossil fuels, combined with the escalation of needs, imposes an unprecedented change of course and a new standard of reference founded on frugality. Economy of energy will not be a calamity for the human race if we consume less but better, giving quality preference over quantity. The coming generations will implement this change, which goes hand in hand with innovation and technological intelligence.

In this field, the hydrogen combustion engine represents hope for humanity and will aid the desired transition if economic and political forces make it a priority.

The equation is simple, although its application may be complex: from the restriction of growth to climate stability, it is the duty of every one of us to make an effort, even if it goes no further than taking care of how we eat. This small contribution by everyone is a prerequisite for a spectacular success by humanity.

PART V
CHALLENGES AND ISSUES
FOR A NEW HUMANISM

· 15 ·
CRISIS IN HEALTH AND SOCIETY

The coronavirus epidemic threatens men and women the world over. The Chinese were the first to diagnose the virus and take radical steps in January 2020 by first protecting the city of Wuhan then rapidly the whole of the country. In spite of its closed borders, the entire world was affected and impacted. Faced with the scale of the spread of the virus, governments–advised by scientists and the World Health Organization–made decisions. Lockdown was decreed a number of times in several countries, without the people being consulted, and this created the conditions for major economic disruption. Some countries, like Sweden or Switzerland, took different paths. People's anxiety grew in proportion to the onslaught of the media, somber faces, and the infection and death counts.

Flashback. At the beginning of the 20th century, one and a half billion people lived together in a food-gathering economy. Better living conditions in the world helped curb epidemics, increased average life expectancy and gave sustainable access to basic necessities–food, water, energy, education and culture.

Our entire system is faltering and wavering because a coronavirus has caused a pandemic. But history reminds us that in the 14th century, the Great Plague, in the space of five years, wiped out nearly half the population of Europe. Numerous pandemics have regularly impacted our societies and new viruses appear constantly. Every year, to general indifference, the flu kills sixty thousand people in Europe and six hundred thousand around the world. The fact that a vaccination is available has not defeated the problem. Deaths due to the effects of malnutrition are also on the rise, caused by deficiencies in essential nutrients or the over-consumption of sugar and animal protein.

Research, access to medical care, the quality of food and water and working conditions have considerably lengthened life spans in richer countries. Never before have human beings enjoyed standards of living so conducive to a fulfilling life. Now a virus is causing chaos, spreading panic around the globe and turning our way of life upside down.

Our society is governed by systems which control and run people's lives. Basic necessities are available in 70 percent of countries, with only Africa and India still lagging behind. Governments have developed protective protocols, which are certainly useful for alerting all the services responsible for detection and the implementation of precautionary measures, but these can turn out to be disproportionate and inefficient. Health has a price, sometimes with a domino effect of serious consequences, especially for the weak and needy. The health crisis has become, by a ripple effect, economic and social.

Overwhelming media coverage and contradictory announcements have caused widespread panic around the world and thrown humanity into a state of emergency and fear. How can people be ordered to stay at home when they can't help needing to go out, to see the doctor, go to the chemist's, purchase food supplies or simply go to work to ensure basic necessities get distributed?

A number of pharmaceutical groups have come up with a vaccine to fight this virus. High-risk segments of the population (the aged, obese and diabetics) and, more generally speaking, those with weakened immunity, are first in line. Others must be able to continue to consciously choose for themselves how they wish to stay healthy.

The progress of science and research, conducted by French and foreign laboratories, should not exclude alternative medicine such as homeopathy. That the cost is no longer reimbursed in France is a mistake, since this form of medicine is very popular, inexpensive and prophylactic. Though there may not be scientific proof of its efficacy, it has nevertheless been well received in France, Switzerland, Germany and many other countries. This method also adopts a holistic and individual approach that complements allopathic medicine. It regards each person as unique, and reacting differently to external aggression but also to disturbances or mental disorders. The aim of this form of medicine is to strengthen a person's system, thereby increasing vitality and resistance to illness.

The principle of dilution is controversial, and homeopathy is disparaged by the scientific community on the grounds that its effectiveness is unverified. However, so-called double-blind tests used to demonstrate the effects of allopathic treatments are not, in this case, suitable, because homeopathy is prescribed and applied differently to each subject on the basis of the fundamental principle that each patient is unique and requires a tailor-made prescription, in particular where serious ailments are concerned. A human being is a whole–mind and body are closely connected and each individual has specificities that demand a tailored response in order to treat the cause of a condition and not just its consequences.

The approach which consists in improving the inner environment of each person's body contributes to limiting the number of illnesses. Prescriptions are often accompanied by nutritional advice as a complement to the treatment. Each person has the basic right to choose which kind of medicine they have faith in, meets their aspirations and keeps them healthy in the long run.

Conventional medicine is approved by means of large-scale clinical tests. It was developed by scientists such as Pasteur, Pierre and Marie Curie and many others who contributed to advances in research. Allopathy adopts a more systematic approach which can call upon the principle of similarity. It is of undeniable interest in fighting many illnesses and especially cancer. The two paths are complementary and guarantee high-end healthcare in all areas to 21st century patients.

This war, this intolerance towards those who offer a different path, must end. All human beings, in their innermost conscience, have the right to live, eat, move around, work and take care of themselves as they wish.

In modern societies, all our leaders are obsessed with precautionary measures. In order to protect themselves from legal and criminal liability, they strive to predict what is unpredictable and to anticipate what should happen.

The past few years have been marked by a major increase in population and life expectancy. In parallel, the various types of cancer have also grown. A stressful lifestyle, an unbalanced diet and pollution are among the main causes. We are witnessing the standardization of diets around vastly increased consumption of animal protein, refined sugars and products rich in artificial additives such as preservatives, colorings and sodium. And yet, the foundation of health is food.

Research by professors such as Vincent Castronovo has brought to light the importance of the gut microbiome, a vital organ for all of us, located in the intestine. Its major role in people's well-being has recently been revealed thanks to the progress of biotechnology. There are more than a hundred thousand billion bacteria in our bodies. Biologically speaking, we can regard ourselves as hybrid, since in and of ourselves we are a population of bacteria, organisms that appeared on planet earth billions of years ago.

If it is inappropriate to criticize the progress of medicine and to question the benefits of research, it would nevertheless be desirable to initiate cool-headed debate on public health and to respect the free will of all, as well as everyone's ability to make the best choice for themselves and their children. Forums that bring together practitioners of different categories should be encouraged, and all topics should be put on the table with transparency, while rejecting the influence of lobbies and cronyism.

The 21st century could be one of well-being and good living. To this end, it is important to carry on facilitating access to education in all countries, continue the improvement of nutrition, and establish a charter for community living based on tolerance, mutual help and respect for nature.

We live in a globalized world which constantly rolls back its limits. Over the past fifty years, human ingenuity has created more wealth, products and innovative services than over the past five millennia.

Nanotechnology and artificial intelligence will profoundly disrupt our habits and intrinsic abilities by changing our priorities and redefining the criteria of our private lives. Human nature needs to create, make discoveries and contribute to further evolution. But this must be done taking into account the limited resources of our planet, respecting individual freedoms and the harmony of nature, and recognizing the climate crisis.

We could envision the creation of a declaration of universal rights and duties in terms of freedom of expression, ethics, sustainable development and societal commitments that would preserve the future of generations to come. It is urgent to stem the headlong forward rush caused by unbridled globalization.

Lockdown impacts human activities and slows pollution on the planet. It will be interesting to see the energy balance and assess its positive consequences in terms of biodiversity. Mother Nature, in her infinite generosity, appreciates this offering made by humanity under constraint, as it sits on the verge of a mental breakdown.

Modern society has created performance. All controlling organizations are established upon calculations and ratios certified by the agencies of global capitalism – Moody's, Standard and Poor's or Fitch ratings. The economic system driven by global stock markets, encourages short-term management and quarterly reports, whereas resilient organization rests upon a long-term approach. The world of finance would be well advised to adapt its model, and take a long-term view of companies and their projects. Hedge funds symbolize the danger of the 21st century, of cash being king and playing with the health of companies listed on the stock market, to the detriment of their strategies and partners. The workforce becomes exhausted and the senior executives of these major groups are put through the wringer by pressure and, in some cases, the absence of stable governance.

We must set greater value on human talent and encourage creativity, risk-taking and lasting performance, as do some family businesses, which are often founded on ethical values and inspire hope and enthusiasm.

This pandemic is only the tip of the iceberg. Other crises will follow, forcing humanity to change and to reconsider the critical issues the planet faces.

A number of voices are being heard that condemn the denials of our current system, particularly the consequences of overexploitation of the riches of the earth. Our environment is going off the rails, threatened by the blindness and selfishness of the richest countries. The desire for change is there, ready to bloom, and will be carried forward by the younger generation, who are more receptive to environmentalism and readier to change their habits.

We must set greater value on human talent and encourage creativity, risk-taking and lasting performance, as do some family businesses, which are often founded on ethical values and inspire hope and enthusiasm.

The real question we ask ourselves today is this: in what world do we wish to live, and what planet do we want to leave our children?

We are only passing through. Nature is eternal, strong yet vulnerable at the same time. We need her–she does not need us.

What are the new models of living together that we wish to establish? What blueprints for governance do we desire? We will need to choose between withdrawing into ourselves and getting nowhere, and a global agreement dedicated to the great topics relevant to humanity: biodiversity, ecological transition, climate, water, health, artificial intelligence, electromagnetic fields, agriculture, energy and demography.

The aim of this declaration will be to respect equilibria and to improve the lives of citizens, with countries, regions and NGOs working closely together.

· 16 ·
BIG BROTHER

Our planet has become a virtual playground where everyone is connected, from New York to Singapore, from Greenland to the Amazonian rain forest, by means of communication satellites and telephones. The changes in the last twenty years are incredible: they represent a quantum leap that has caused an upheaval in the way the world is organized. The development of the Internet and the power of the communication networks have changed the priorities of human beings.

The American Big Five corporations, GAFAM (Google, Apple, Facebook, Amazon and Microsoft), will soon be joined by their Chinese challengers Alibaba and Huawei and the South Korean Samsung. These groups, which are more powerful than states, have developed search systems, software and applications which surpass the needs of humanity. Transhumanism, robots and artificial intelligence are no longer figments of the imagination of those visionary novelists of past decades who attempted to foresee the world of tomorrow. Today's reality far eclipses fiction.

It has always been like this. Things that seemed unimaginable and no more than fantasy, such as going *Round the World in Eighty Days* as in Jules Verne's tale, have now been accomplished and immeasurably bettered. Records are broken one after another by racing yachts, sailed by skippers armed with technology and unlimited data and assisted by route planners to set the best course, without even leaving their cabins. The human adventure is now pre-planned, events are prepared in minute detail, precisely timed and predicted. Data is integral to the management of any project. In team sports, video analysts and statisticians now play a major role in the run-up to a match. With larger teams of interchangeable players at their disposal, coaches have increased power and use their teams predictively instead of intuitively. Empiricism, discovery and creative freedom have been superseded by meticulous preparation, preestablished action plans and repeated combinations.

In the economic field, statistics are used to analyze market share, progress, trends and consumer behavior patterns. The large international retail corporations have abandoned their original trade as shopkeepers in favor of that of managers. Stores have become sterile self-service areas where 90 percent of the stock is the same from one country to another.

All jobs in the service sector are in a state of flux. The banks provide insurance and the insurers open banks and offer loans. The most striking changes result from the boom in online shopping and the shifts in the purchasing habits of consumers. The latter are classified into different categories: the *millennials*, in the 18 to 35 age group, are the favorite target group of the admen as the roving consumers of today and tomorrow, whose consumption habits are not those of their parents. The world has become a huge Monopoly board on which the jackpot can be won very quickly.

The hyper-creative accounting and blindness of some bankers led to the crash of 2008, the culmination of a cycle that began in the 2000s, originating with a circle restricted to an elite speaking a highly specific jargon that very few corporate managers understand. A thick smokescreen enveloped Manhattan, Shanghai, London, Tokyo and Paris. The bankruptcy of Lehmann Brothers created chaos and threw the global economy into a temporary recession; the lessons were learned, however, enabling stricter rules of governance to be introduced.

When capital income brings in more money than investment in production, the economy is in serious trouble. The market capitalization of the largest corporations, especially those with links to new technologies and services, defies the imagination. The real value of Uber bears no relation to its earnings. But losses do not discourage investors, who bet on the reliability of their "disruptive" models.

When capital income brings in more money than investment in production, the economy is in serious trouble.

In the world of high tech, there is no place for pessimism, because the new companies innovate and turn established concepts upside down. The successful book *Stratégie Océan bleu*, by W. Chan Kim and Renée Mauborgne[1], researchers at INSEAD, shows that when companies create a new demand they necessarily also create more space for growth and profit than those competing in a sphere that already exists.

The problems that come with the new information systems reside in the way people have come to depend on their electronic terminal and organize their professional and personal life around it. Private life has become an outdated concept. We are all analyzed, ranked and tested. Connectivity and updates are the favorite playground of artificial intelligence.

The labor market will soon become a theater of collaboration between human beings, connected objects and robots, which will force workers to retrain continually or become disqualified.

The menace of digital dictatorship is on our doorstep. It threatens to take the place of our logical process of decision and risk-taking,

---

[1] Pearson, 2010.

curtailing freedom and creating atrociously inegalitarian societies ordered by a restricted elite. According to *Forbes* magazine, the fortune of the six hundred richest North Americans has grown by fifteen percent during the Covid-19 crisis, an increase of four hundred and thirty-four billion dollars.

Big Data has become a bonanza in which we have all been transformed from customers into products. Our behaviors, emotions and messages are recorded and sold for advertising purposes in the interval before algorithms do the deciding and make our purchases on our behalf. The collection and use of data, its exchange and resale, have become one of the most important challenges of our civilization. We are continuously contacted and we receive vast numbers of messages containing suggestions for a destination, a product or a forthcoming event. The proliferation of "marketplaces" shortens distances, favoring the emergence of digital platforms of unrivaled power.

The Chinese have protected their domestic market of 1.4 billion people by prohibiting the entry of American multinationals and giving preference to large Chinese groups such as Alibaba and Tencent.

Social media networks have interconnected the entire planet, and those who had fought to defend their identity and their secret garden are the first to display their lives on all the fashionable platforms. The world has become schizophrenic. We observe increasing rates of disturbed behavior, strong addictions and lost points of reference as the frontier between the real and virtual worlds begins to blur. Three-D experiences are so sophisticated that their users quickly lose their sense of reality. Yet these new systems have promoted the spread of information all over the world. Some totalitarian countries still block access to a free Internet, but this cannot last. The prophecy that all will be revealed is coming true, for better or worse. Filters are disappearing, and press releases are often software-generated.

Nevertheless, the publication of information has put an end to a number of dictatorships. The period of the Arab Spring was very significant and changed society in those countries. It also helped us to realize that democracy is not the result of a popular tidal wave, but a concept that must be tested and must meet the requirements of organization, morals and politics.

The market economy fosters innovation and the steady emergence of new products. Fifty percent of those that will be available to us ten years from now do not yet exist. Technological competition is in full swing.

It is important that production companies should establish an international pricing corridor able to overcome the problems caused by customs duties in order to reduce the inequalities between different distribution channels, because consumers compare the prices of consumer products.

We have entered a civilization of leisure, with a wealth of choice. Time accelerates and space shrinks. Technology is everywhere, in every corner of our lives. Online sales are quickly gaining market share at the expense of purchases in stores, and have considerably changed certain industries. Fashion, luxury and cosmetics have adopted this sales model as a baseline of their "business model". Retailers are in competition with the brands. We have moved from a retail model to an integrated model. These changes profoundly modify purchasing behavior. The younger generations buy most of their clothes online. The leading groups develop sales areas known as "showrooms" where people can identify the specifics of the brand and buy its products. The successes of such names as Zara or H & M are examples of integration.

The proliferation of digital platforms has generated considerable needs for human resources trained in the construction of these ecosystems. The geeks of Silicon Valley or China, and of Asian countries in general, have built up a considerable lead over Europe.

On the military front, research has achieved considerable progress in the geolocation of enemies and strategic sites, and attacking them using drones. Power relationships between countries have been drastically altered. Technology limits the loss of human life where the great powers are concerned.

We are living in a fascinating period for creativity and the production of content. We can watch fashion parades on our telephones. Television channels have proliferated and video has become the most popular form of expression on the Internet. The coronavirus lockdown crisis has generated large numbers of virtual conferences. Instagram Live is now the place for dialogue and listening to concerts by our favorite performers.

In the world of music, sites devoted to streaming have taken the place of traditional record stores. The music industry, after struggling for ten years, has gotten its second wind. iTunes, YouTube and Spotify have brought unlimited free access to all who want to listen to music. Their paid premium services offer incentives, exclusive issues and previews. Algorithms give you suggestions for music that matches your tastes. TV shows have gone down the same road: Netflix has altered the habits of numerous viewers, who may spend an evening binge-watching an addictive series like *Game of Thrones* or *House of Cards*. The episodes are short and content-dense.

The human brain is bombarded non-stop with images, sounds, vibrations and text messages containing information. As a consequence, young people's attention spans have declined. They have trouble concentrating, as their minds have grown used to continually switching from one demand to the next. Some discipline needs to be injected into this lifestyle before it deteriorates into delusion and alienation.

New technologies accentuate the materialism and heartlessness of present-day society, the verbal violence, the rising flood of true and fake news, the sensationalism of the media. It is a tidal wave that causes anxiety and trivializes suffering. Each news item is supplanted by the next. Living has become anxiety-inducing, especially for people living in big cities who have lost contact with the power and beauty of nature.

The current mode of organization reinforces dependence on the system. But awareness, generosity and goodwill derive from independence. We are saturated with the virtual world, and its excesses contribute to loneliness and emotional bankruptcy. By seeking a new balance, we will regain our creative capacities and our innate affinity for connecting with other people.

· 17 ·
LIFE LESSONS

The human body is a sanctuary. It is our vehicle, continuously changing from the moment of our conception, through birth, childhood, adolescence, adulthood, maturity, old age and until death. It is unique, its DNA, cells, organs, flesh, bones and brain make it a living, vibrant entity.

We can identify the physical, etheric and astral bodies, the trinity establishing the link between the mind, spirit and soul. Each person's aura is unique, we all radiate with different intensities and colors that vary according to our state of physical health, consciousness and superconsciousness. The physical dimension is essential because it makes the conditions for a pleasant life possible, provided we take care of ourselves. Health is the gateway to a successful daily life.

Food is the vital fuel for our body. Our increasingly sedentary and urban lifestyle has radically changed our consumer habits and the quality of the products we ingest. Food safety has contributed to establishing standards and calibrating food items ensuring food products are distributed year-round. Supermarkets, those consumer temples, offer tens of thousands of products unrestricted by seasonality. The share of processed foods, ready to eat or drink, is ever greater. Increasingly, consumer choices are guided by advertising, special offers and trends, to the detriment of the seasons, traditions and local produce. The success of this type of commerce lies in its practicality, its aggressive pricing and its constant adjustments to preserve customer loyalty. The emergence of the drive-through and the development of online sales have allowed the homemaker to spend less and less time in the shops. The major investments on the part of big brands and specialty retailers like Amazon or Alibaba guarantee shipping in record time.

Our way of life and living standards have nevertheless caused a greater awareness of the need to feed ourselves better, with products from the local land or organically farmed. Following the long-standing efforts of organic farmers and activists, the breakthrough occurred thanks to specialist chains, and is now spreading to all distribution sectors. The two major challenges for our food and health are the quality of products and the variety in our diets.

Intensive farming offers a supply of healthy, standardized products to sixty percent of the inhabitants of the planet. For the others, low income, poor living conditions or inadequate distribution networks lead to a diet comprised mainly of local produce, grains and seasonal vegetables.

Africa is the continent suffering the most from malnutrition. Western countries, in particular North America and Europe, consume to excess: their inhabitants suffer from obesity and cardiovascular diseases. Asia, and especially Japan, can be a role model in terms of products beneficial to health. The balance of the diet that characterizes this continent guarantees a sufficient supply of calories while being relatively low in carbs and meat but rich in omega 3.

The diet of the Mediterranean also deserves attention. It is none other than the dietary lifestyle followed by humble people for thousands of years. The staples of this diet are an abundance of seasonal fruits and vegetables, olive oil, a wholesome balance between cereals, seafood products and meat, and a glass of wine per meal for adults. Americans, who seem to be fond of miraculous diet plans, call it simply the *Mediterranean diet* and associate it with another dietary oddity they name the *French paradox*-The French paradox is the question of how the French, who drink wine, eat cheese and foie gras but also fresh and seasonal produce, have lower rates of heart disease.

Food is the bedrock of our health and the respect we owe our bodily vehicle. Sports and physical exercise also play a major role in our emotional stability. The education systems of certain countries, particularly in northern Europe, encourage their daily practice. The foundation acquired during childhood and adolescence, particularly a taste for physical effort, contributes to growing up harmoniously. The power and endurance acquired through sports and the enjoyment in testing one's limits open the doors to a better knowledge of our body and its potential, and strengthen self-confidence.

There needs to be a balance between calories absorbed and calories spent. The primary role of a doctor should be that of an advisor who, instead of prescribing medication, would coach patients towards a balanced lifestyle. The paradox of the 21st century is that we live, on average, longer, by taking more and more medication. France, whose social welfare system is one of the most supportive in the world, is the best example of this. We use more pharmaceutical products than our neighbors.

More widespread nutritional advice enables better management of our food habits and therefore of our state of wellness. Dr. Kousmine advocates the three pillars of "a king's breakfast, a prince's lunch and a pauper's dinner". Chrononutrition promotes both health and restful sleep. It requires discipline if we are to enjoy disregarding it from time to time.

The most important thing is to be able to listen to, and moderate, our needs by distancing ourselves from compulsive urges. The circulation of energies in our body, good endurance and stable mental balance are the keys to a harmonious life.

We have emphasized the physical dimension of the body, sustained by nutrition and exercise. The second level of consciousness opens the doors of the spiritual dimension to us. *"Mens sana in corpore sano"*, wrote Juvenal – a healthy mind in a healthy body. To listen to one's body, to be aware of it but also to stimulate and regulate it by the power of thought. When practiced first thing in the morning, active breathing, stretching, and close observation of our heartbeat make a good start to the day and stimulate creative thought. Stress, insomnia and aggression hamper personal fulfillment.

The increasing digitalization of our life makes moments of calm and inner peace rarer. In this virtual world, the younger generations end up forgetting their uniqueness. The virtual universe, with its social networks, Internet and video games, acts as a powerful sedative, cutting human beings off from their individuality, intimate connection to their fellows and the macrocosm.

When practiced first thing in the morning, active breathing, stretching, and close observation of our heartbeat make a good start to the day and stimulate creative thought.

The rapid rise of a select few in reality television, music or sport, mediatized by the big communication groups, sets the bar very high for young people desperate for heroes and conformity. Self-esteem, the doorway to a successful life as a mature adult, becomes hard to attain, because the expectations of present-day society are very high. It is therefore vital, for the human beings of our new era, to embark upon a journey of self-discovery. Which includes parental education, studies and, for some, religion. Culture and reading are essential in order to understand the evolution of humanity and situate ourselves in time and space.

From the Big Bang to the present day, the universe has been expanding. Lifting our gaze to the heavens, taking the time to meditate and contemplate in silence the wonders of creation will open the gates of a new paradigm of mindful awareness in which each person will understand that the power of the mind and our thoughts is the basis of a life in which we thrive and flourish. We cannot have faith in others if we do not have faith in ourselves – it is vital to extend loving kindness to oneself in order to do so to others. We grow each day as soon as fear leaves our hearts, to be replaced by the human adventure and new human connections in search of new experiences.

Religions can bring people together, beyond schools of thought and beliefs, in a respectful and generous environment. Faith in a higher power both calms and stimulates the mind. Tribalism, sectarianism and the culture of ostracism must give way to universalism. We are all children of God and we must give of our best to protect nature, the environment, family and our neighbor. Faith is essential because it develops human consciousness beyond what is perceivable and comprehensible. The connection to sentient and supersentient worlds, understanding other forms of belief and a thirst for knowledge assist spiritual awakening which, throughout our lives, step by step, day after day, guides our path.

Quantum physics sheds new light on the concept of immortality of the soul, which remains one of the mysteries of humanity.

The British physicists Roger Penrose and Stephen Hawking jointly formulated the hypothesis that information is stored after death in microtubules on the quantum and subatomic scale. This would mean that after the body dies, consciousness lives on in a universe of a different nature which we cannot perceive on a material level but only on a spiritual one.

In metaphysics, mind transcends matter. By broadening the field of all possibilities, the body, mind and soul harmonize, helping us to better understand our closeness, our potential and our connection to others and the universe.

· 18 ·
NEW CHALLENGES FOR RELIGIONS

There are nearly ten thousand religions in the world, but the four largest ones, Christianity, Hinduism, Islam and Buddhism, are practiced by the great majority of human beings. Schisms and dissension have sometimes split them into subgroups. Islam is divided into four branches (Sunni, Shia, Zaidiyyah and Ibadi) and Protestantism in the 16th century gave rise to a new movement and, in our day, to various different churches (Lutherans, Presbyterians, Jehovah's Witnesses, Seventh Day Adventists, and others).

This spiritual exuberance has contributed to structuring human life around education and fixed settlements with a cleric as authority figure and family advisor. Religious zeal and the networking of territories have proposed answers to fundamental and metaphysical questions. Shamanism in South America, Asia and Africa and Shintoism in Japan have become widely acknowledged traditions. The main religions developed proselytism.

This task was assumed by religious organizations, but also by armies, giving rise for centuries on end to terrible battles and bloody conquests in the name of God.

More recently, missionaries have used diplomacy and persuasion to develop Christian teachings around the world. This method of recruitment is also the *modus operandi* of Islam and Buddhism.

Eighty percent of the inhabitants of our planet have received a religious education and belong, to a greater or lesser degree, to such a community. Rates of observance and attendance at services vary widely. Islam, with its routine of daily prayers, displays a very high level of devotion and practices purification of the body with the fast of Ramadan and daily ablutions. The Christian fast of Lent is much less widely observed in our day. In Judaism, the traditional celebrations of the Passover and Yom Kippur are the most popular. In all religions, we must distinguish between religious services which bring the faithful nearer to God by intercession, and personal prayer, which establishes a direct, intimate relationship with the Creator.

Various approaches can be adopted to connect with the mystery of spiritual elevation. Monotheistic religions offer the path of prayer, collective or individual, in order to seek and sense this extracorporeal presence. In Hinduism, mantras lead to Brahma. Buddhism demands an ascetic practice that drives self-development by means of relaxation and meditation in order to attain a state of inner peace.

Prayer is transcendent and connects us to the divine spirit, and meditation produces a sense of fulfillment: both approaches facilitate elevation and nurture humankind's ability to better understand the meaning of life.

For five thousand years, *Homo sapiens* has been developing cognitive capacities essential to greater comprehension of the causality of his existence. The deeper purpose of each person's life, the vital force and self-knowledge enable an existential quest, broaden the field of possibilities and assert individuality, personality and the ability to grasp the duality between the temporal and spiritual spheres.

These two jurisdictions are nowadays separate in the majority of countries. In the Middle Ages, however, the church wielded power extending into the temporal world. This dark age can serve as a reminder of all conflicts of interest and the obscurantism of all religious extremes, such as fanaticism and fundamentalism. The recent terror attacks committed by radical Islamists stigmatize a religion and school of thought which condemn such acts.

The time has come for humanity to unite in advocating for a coming together of peoples, ethnic groups and communities in a movement of tolerance, solidarity and opening of hearts. The issue is not to trivialize beliefs or religious convictions but rather, in a constantly changing world, to define a common, foundational and universalistic frame of reference. Every religion should preach peace, love, respect, charity, life in society, freedom of expression, kindness, justice and dignity.

The 21st century could become one in which bridges are built between religions and philosophical movements to create a new paradigm which invites prayer, mediation and dialogue, without taboo, fear or suspicion. Interfaith encounters are still too few and far between. Each community protects its certainties, its culture and its rites without creating any openings, a state of affairs that should be inconceivable if we go back to the roots of the three main monotheistic religions and their offshoots, of which Abraham is the founding father. The Bible, in the Old and New testaments, tells the story of these nomadic tribes, and this biblical narrative covers four thousand years of history, culture and conquests. In the same period, for two thousand years, the wisdom contributed by Greek philosophy, the development of reasoning and a happy outlook contributed to the advent of a more organized world and a view of an ideal society.

The temporal and spiritual worlds, things secular and sacred, reason and ideals are concepts favorable to this tremendous forward surge of humanity. In 18th-century France, the Lumières movement developed a philosophical knowledge and a cultural effervescence that spread right across Europe. This rivalry culminated, in France, in the Revolution and the establishment of secularism, freedom of conscience and individual rights. The separation of Church and State opened up new horizons for all.

Twenty percent of humans remain atheist or agnostic, but increasing numbers are questioning and reviewing the meaning and priorities of life.

The relationship to work differs depending on the country but also on age. There is often a rift between the younger generations and their elders, as the former break earlier with parental supervision in terms of education and culture. Ethics is a sensitive topic, as is the protection of the environment. Family structures are also evolving with the emergence of new lifestyles: celibacy, single-parent families and retirement homes for senior citizens.

Spirituality and religious practice have not escaped change. Sometimes, tradition gives way to experience and inquiry. Meditation workshops, the regular practice of fasting and spiritual retreats have become resoundingly successful, particularly with overworked *We must use our experience to prepare a new paradigm founded on love, sensitivity and spirituality* people seeking a new equilibrium. The concept of autonomy and the development of consciousness assist the evolution of sensitive and intuitive people and their personal development, to improve life on our planet.

This temporal opening causes tensions and fierce struggles between the partisans of yesterday's world and those of tomorrow's.

We live in the eternal present: we must use our experience to prepare a new paradigm founded on love, sensitivity and spirituality, and put an end to the current mechanisms of domination based on fear, egoism, self-centeredness and materialism.

The present paradox resides in the rift between the people and their governing bodies, exacerbated by the flow of unverified and unauthenticated information. The best and the worst is disseminated via social networks at lightning speed and without filters. Human beings need both temporal and spiritual reference points. Both are linked, because standards of living influence people's mental and psychological state in the long term.

Peace of mind comes with disciplined practice, a positive attitude and inner exploration. It is personal work that requires diligence in order to achieve lasting happiness. The globalized and interconnected world we live in is increasingly aggressive, invasive and violent. There is urgency everywhere, in all areas. Mobile phones, tablets, and computers connected to networks and Wi-Fi have taken over the time for idleness or introspection that is necessary to regain harmony, compassion and depth of feelings.

This information overload, wave fields, and the pressure generated by belonging to one or more real or virtual communities throw our contemporaries off balance, especially the new generations born into these new technologies. This alienation and waning of the desire for transcendence, calm and inner peace create internal chaos, stress and more recently a new condition known as burnout. The proliferation of communication networks requires of us restraint and a raised level of consciousness so that each person may organize their life serenely.

Breathing techniques prepare one for meditation and awakening.

Individual and group prayers develop consciousness and supersentience, connecting one's being to cosmic energies.

Life is a constant challenge offering surprises and sometimes unexpected encounters for those who cultivate positive thinking, volition, the impulse of the heart and love for their fellows. This personal quest is the path of truth, genuine joy and shared happiness.

· 19 ·
NEW CHALLENGES FOR POLITICS

Power relationships between countries are shifting. We are moving from bilateralism into multilateralism. In 1957, a small group of European countries created the EEC, a community whose founding principles established economic cooperation between France, West Germany, Belgium, Italy, Luxembourg and the Netherlands. Before long, in 1967, it was enlarged to twelve countries. In 2009, the EEC became the European Union, which brought together twenty-seven countries in a region inhabited by five hundred million people, with a common currency, the Euro, for most of its members.

Its economic power is considerable, despite the recent departure of the United Kingdom, with 37 percent of its transactions. Colossus though it is, it is founded on a fragile foundation, in disharmony with the sovereignty of its states.

In military terms, the radical reduction of European budgets has strengthened the leadership of the United States and China, giving them free rein to exercise their growing influence on every continent.

The financial situation of some states, such as Greece, and the failure to control budget deficits alarm the markets and the experts. The advantageous social security systems created in the 1970s have suffered from budget cuts and an increase in the debt of many countries, in excess of 100 percent of GDP. The recent Covid-19 crisis amplifies the economic shock wave and could land Europe in a lasting recession if bold, solidarity-based, long-term measures are not provided for.

The world of the 21st century is founded on a global economy whose perpetual advance is designed to favor growth, international competition and the circulation of goods and services, supported by ever more complex financial systems and control mechanisms dominated by ultramodern technology. This model, which it was thought nothing and no one could restrain, has foundered because of a virus that appeared without warning and whose future consequences cannot yet be predicted.

Will this momentous event, comparable to the great crash of 1929 or the oil price shock of the 1970s, mark the onset of a decline of the current model, or will it use different methods, based this time on proven industrial assets and disruptive technological innovation?

Global growth has contracted decisively during the pandemic, heralding a historic impact on the economies of the planet and a violent reaction which will convulse our professional, social and cultural systems. Will this momentous event, comparable to the great crash of 1929 or the oil price shock of the 1970s, mark the onset of a decline of the current model, or will it use different methods, based this time on proven industrial assets and disruptive technological innovation?

The ultraliberal principles of the present market economy are based on multilateral deals facilitated and upheld by the Word Trade Organization. This growth model is only effective if it functions at full capacity, because the analytical and support criteria of the banking institutions are guided by the principles of short-term yield. For the last forty years, the liberalization of world trade in combination with the withdrawal of the welfare state has boosted progressive mechanisms, favoring a dramatic increase in global wealth but also its ill-proportioned distribution, engendering private empires that are more powerful than many countries.

The regulation and control of the economy by state governments have become an illusion. In many countries it is multinationals that provide the circulation of capital and innovation, especially in technology, without any control whatsoever. The speed with which these intrusive technologies evolve promises human beings a fantastic vision of immortality. It is true that science and research have succeeded in solving many of the world's problems and have brought better access to treatment and medicines, in conformity with perpetually improving health criteria. But the other side of the coin is that in this unrestrained rush for more and more, the notion of the common good and the vital connection between humankind and nature are neither taken into account nor respected. Pollution of the seas, deforestation, diets ever richer in protein and the continuing increase in hydrocarbon use have destroyed the subtle balances of Planet Earth and the harmony vital to the renewal of resources and sustainable development. The disruption of the climate is the consequence of human activity and of revolutionary decisions, their consequences intensified by the illusion of immediate success.

Some states are tempted to confront their problems individually on the basis of populist, demagogic ideas that are easier to communicate politically and are calculated to win electoral success.

The selfishness of some rulers, backed by the necessity to get results, alienates the decision makers and paralyzes the multinational institutions. Their silence is accentuated by the speed of operation of the markets, stock price volatility and the excessive financialization of the world, acting under the influence of tools of control that are beyond most people's understanding.

Precautionary principles inhibit any bold and original initiative by our leaders, obstinate in their determination to adhere to the standards and conventions laid down by such bodies as the World Trade Organization, the United Nations or the World Health Organization. In peaceful times and when conditions are favorable, these regulatory systems ensure economic stability and public health. But in circumstances of recession or pandemic, they prevent all empirical action required by the emergency. We are witnesses of a legislative stranglehold on society that discourages any initiative in the absence of scientific guarantees, which in some cases are impossible to obtain.

This is a time of exceptional gravity for the future of our species. The population explosion, improvements in living conditions and longer life expectancy have caused a surge in individual and collective needs. The planet cannot provide the resources demanded by this frenzy without drawing on its reserves. It is therefore vitally necessary to set out a hierarchy of human needs that takes the state of the planet into account, within the framework of a system capable of providing good guidelines for being and living.

Politics must regain its etymological and philosophical meaning to redefine the way life on earth is organized and imagine a new mode of governance, more open and harmonious. Unrestrained growth can no longer be the guiding principle of our society, because it fails to meet present needs and cannot cope with the climate emergency and the loss of biodiversity. Nothing but a resilient system will be able to usher in a new era for humankind.

Systems of domination have revealed their limitations, because we all live in an interdependent world where inequalities create the conditions for rebellion and mass migrations. The decisions being made at present on the economic, social and climatic levels are insufficient to restore the equilibrium of the planet.

Bold multigenerational commitments pursuing the common good must involve all the countries in the world. This generous proposal will lay down guiding principles incorporating equality of opportunity, respect for difference, biodiversity and the marine world, but also the freedom of the individual, food, renewed local production of basic necessities, harmony of towns, a balance between labor and capital, redistribution of value chains, a sense of innovation and levels of awareness. Equality of opportunity between the people of the South and the North, rich countries and poor countries, will be achieved through access to education for all and prospects for personal and professional development in symbiosis with each person's aspirations, talents and willpower. Respect for difference will foster the ability of all to achieve self-fulfillment and build up a local, national and international community united by a shared destiny in harmony with our incarnation and our mission in this world.

Giving meaning to their lives is the goal desired by every person in this world. This transcendental yearning will open the way to a new paradigm, which may seem utopian today, but could be achieved tomorrow. Planet Earth is suffering from the abuse inflicted on her by the ongoing onslaughts due to human activity. Nature is stronger and more intelligent than we are. She has fostered the growth of humanity and, in her unbounded generosity, has given us the resources and energy that were needed for our development.

Numerous climatic warnings have recently impacted several continents. If mankind closes its ears to this suffering, more problems will follow, viral, bacterial or cataclysmic.

Biodiversity is a treasure house for future generations: it must be protected and restored. Respect for the animal and plant world is crucial to ensuring harmony on the planet. Every species and every plant has its unique part to play in this symphony of the world. Disruptions lead to chain reactions throughout the hierarchy: from the microbes in the soil and subsoil to every living being.

Nature is self-sufficient and self-regulating. To understand the interactions between living things is to accept with humility that humankind is only one component in a perfectly organized natural whole, interconnected with the solar system and the entire universe.

The seas and ocean currents play a fundamental role in feeding the human race and influencing the winds and the climate. Rivers and streams are also essential for providing abundant water for every human being, irrigating crops and enabling riverine transport. Their fauna also contributes to our food supply.

Forests are the lungs of the planet. They provide long-term carbon storage, maintain biodiversity and make possible the life of the wild animals and insects that form part of the prodigious organization that surrounds us.

The political world is under a duty to give protected status to our natural habitats by an equitable international agreement, with long-term financial incentives for leaving certain zones unexploited by human activity. It is easy to criticize the decisions made by the leaders of a few countries, in present-day Amazonia, for instance, or in the near future in Alaska. But what do we propose instead, and how can we structure equitable compensation for each country corresponding to unexploited wealth on the ground, underground or in the sea? The twenty richest countries should set the example by proposing an ambitious program, generous and protective, that will offer compensation to the rest of humanity.

The current model, materialist and skewed, has run out of steam. It has no option but to change and propose a new system of organization for the eight billion humans living on this planet, integrating the principles of tolerance and individual freedom. Respect for every individual and every country, with freedom of self-determination within common rules, must take priority. Security must never be an excuse for the sacrifice of hard-won liberties, often obtained at the cost of human lives, throughout past centuries. These heroes battled totalitarian systems, abolished slavery and defined the rights and duties of all.

A new chapter could cover the rights of humankind and of nature. The latter has given unstintingly: it is time for the human race to repay its debt to her and, in an inversion of priorities, restore her to her pre-eminent position.

Eating, too, is a political act, repeated two or three times every day. In every choice that we make when we buy food and drink, we are influenced by current trends. Our conditioning by advertising and price must give way to a preference for products that respect a chain of values between producers, artisans and retailers, and adhere to an ethical specification that promotes the respect of soils, biodiversity, nutritional quality and recyclable packaging. Sustainable, organic or biodynamic labels will give the consumer quality guarantees. The relocation of agriculture to the peripheral areas around large cities would also ensure better quality at a reasonable price, while supply logistics would have a limited carbon footprint.

Food supplies should be a national priority everywhere, with at least 70 percent self-sufficiency the norm.

New towns should not copy the model of the gigantic, dehumanized megalopolis, but must be more integrated and take nature into consideration. New York, London, Paris, Shanghai, Tokyo or Sydney are symbols of modernity which have now been transformed by the coronavirus crisis into places of bare survival, due to their failure to respect biodiversity and their unsuitability for integrated farming.

Over the last twenty years, the capital-labor ratio has shifted by 10 percent in favor of the former. Several factors have accelerated this disparity: improvements in techniques and technological advances have propagated robotization of tasks to the detriment of human involvement. The same thing has been happening in office applications and the field of machine tools, with computerization and communication networks.

The privatization of state-owned companies inescapably detaches states from their production facilities and weakens their independence, especially in the sectors of power, water and operating systems for confidential use.

The enormous disparity between the minimum wage and the highest salaries has aggravated inequality and is a threat to social cohesion. The liberalization of the economy has enabled significant advances and beneficial changes in the industrialized countries in the last fifty years. However, its excesses must be corrected by the determination of governments to regulate operations and look after the workers of their countries, who are the guarantors of national unity, especially in times of crisis. Strategic sectors, such as the armed services and energy, but also legal and financial institutions, are valuable goods and services which deserve staff who are qualified, expert and motivated, and must therefore be well paid. Recruiting talented people to work in the administrative machinery of a country is vital for its proper operation, the confidence it inspires and the exemplary quality of the service it provides.

Unbridled global competition has resulted in the concentration of companies, often boosted by stock market prices and occurring through complex capital mechanisms. At the beginning of its cycle, every company has made use of its dynamism and innovative ideas to develop, but has also been favored by the domestic market of its country which has helped it to grow. Internationalization and the development of subsidiaries abroad are good and necessary, provided the companies concerned continue to pay their taxes in their country of origin and elsewhere. Tax exile is not appropriate, and falsifies the competition between large groups and family concerns. Capital is necessary and desirable for economic development as long as it is ethical, and is used generously and in the service of the greater good. In a number of countries around the world, better distribution of income has been made possible by schemes involving financial participation, incentives and bonuses, especially to maintain the life force of companies or to attract the most talented workers in their preferred sectors.

Unskilled workers are threatened by machines in every sector. These people must be assisted and given time to train, and the younger ones must be guided towards apprenticeships and work-study contracts, which often lead to a first job.

The slump in purchasing power and the dissatisfaction of the working classes are often bound up with the social breakdown and excesses caused by unbridled capitalism. As a general rule, employees have a sense of involvement in the life of their companies, to which they develop a strong emotional attachment. They are proud and happy to participate in a human adventure that brings them their daily bread, gives structure to their professional life and creates a social bond and a feeling of belonging. For these reasons, they do not easily tolerate injustices, especially the brutality of unexplained and unjust decisions such as closures or relocation.

France is one of the countries with the most generous social security support. Other more liberal countries do not provide the same mitigating mechanisms in times of crisis. The unemployment rate is no more than an indicator of work levels and hence of the job market. The labor-capital combination must be as resilient and balanced as possible, in harmony with human beings and nature, and no longer steered by the over-financialization of the economy.

The concept of progress should be reexamined in the light of the re-humanization of our existing models. This pervasive change must not be systematically correlated with performance, because progress needs to be measured over the long term. For example, the transformation of intensive agriculture into an organic model is an act of militant social responsibility which, while it does not promise short-term financial gain, offers a transition bringing values and meaning to the managers, shareholders and employees of a business. These changes represent human and social progress and must be encouraged and reproduced.

Blind competition exhausts teams and systems too. An enlightened view of a different, more altruistic future creates the conditions favorable to happiness. Innovation has often been the driving force of growth, because it anticipates coming needs and brings lasting change to society.

Thirty years ago, the Research and Development departments of the large international groups, especially those of Silicon Valley, introduced digital communication, functioning through super-powerful databases and connected to everyone through mobile telephones. This made progress possible in many areas, especially the fields of information technology, medicine, space research and the economy.

Recently developed experimental prototypes, the appearance of nanotechnology and the collection of personal data are bringing us to the threshold of transhumanism. The ethical dimension will very soon be one of the central preoccupations of human beings.

Must we allow governments, whose interests are often tied up with those of major groups, to determine the development of research and, as a result, impose the proliferation of data transfer by satellites, antennas and networks of every kind and consequently the centralization of the data contained in our phones? Must individual liberty be sacrificed on the altar of security? Will our personal data, health records and genetic sequences be accessible to our banks, insurance companies and police forces? All these existential questions are at the heart of the problems facing us today. The climate and health crises may be exacerbated by an additional identity crisis. Politics must be ethical and at the service of everyone. The numerous social questions currently making headlines clearly indicate the need to reinvent the system.

The duality between good and evil, light and darkness, the spiritual and the material, intuition and intelligence, is the province of philosophical and transcendental debates that are vital in the historic period in which we live. We have reached a stage where all things are possible. There is still time to construct a society where human beings, in harmony with nature and in pleasant surroundings, will live stable, caring lives. In contrast, the aggression and brutality of our present-day world pose the risk of profound dehumanization as connected objects take over control of our minds and our freedom of choice.

The gravity of the situation and the extent of the crisis must restore good sense and political courage to those who govern our planet, who cannot avoid coming to a global agreement on the fundamental subjects shared by all nations.

This raising of awareness of issues and priorities can be represented diagrammatically like this:

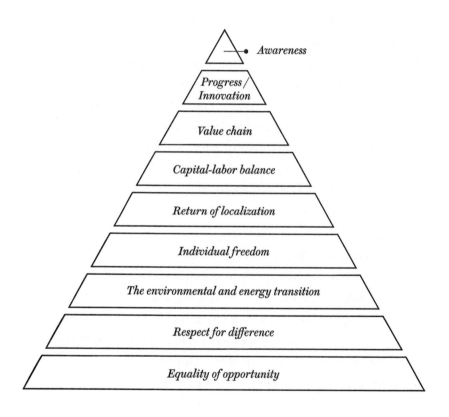

• PYRAMID OF A BETTER WORLD •

·20·
A NEW PARADIGM

The universe is expanding and reminds us of our condition as human beings, incarnated and limited by the time-bound vehicle that is our body. Over thousands of years, evolution–Darwin's brainchild–has given us ever greater abilities, and humanity's level of consciousness has continuously fueled a constant quest both for knowledge and an understanding of physical and metaphysical phenomena, as well as of the interaction between nature and living beings. More recently, mathematicians and scientists have discovered the perfection of creation and the fact that everything obeys numerical laws and is in harmony. This eternal pattern of organization already existed before the appearance of human beings on earth. The precise mechanics of the universe, the galaxies and our solar system, is an absolute demonstration of a higher, regulating power.

The Vitruvian Man, drawn by Leonardo da Vinci in 1490, offers perfect dimensions inside a square or a circle. This emblematic allegory positions man at the center of everything. He rests on a magnificent pedestal magnified by the laws of the universe. The same harmony can be found in music: there are twelve notes in an octave and twelve major harmonics between two octave notes. This works out at a total of one hundred and forty-four different combinations.

The flower of life is the most harmonious and most organized drawing of creation, as it contains all the laws of physics and mathematics and symbolizes the universe and the perfection of creation. It can also be defined as a three-part structure, space, time and matter. The complexity of our universe puts us in our place and makes us humble, but also generates an overwhelming desire for knowledge, progress and personal expansion.

The current era is pushing back the limits of our understanding and perception, by establishing connections between *Homo sapiens* and computers. The power of computation of the latter foreshadows a new world in which algorithms and artificial intelligence will attempt to seize power. This era of conscious computers will create a different relationship between man and machines and a partnership that will reveal all the mysteries of life. It will then be possible to understand one's DNA, predict one's life span, and also choose the gender of one's child. Humans will manufacture intergalactic ships enabling them to travel unrestricted by current space-time.

But the visceral need for discovery and exploration will replace neither the feelings nor the emotions that we experience and which connect us. Similarly, the quest for immortality will meet with resistance from life itself, which has meaning only because it is finite.

The best and the worst are here, calling out to us and inviting us to raise our level of consciousness and prepare a world offering the possibility of transcendence and awakening, not just hedonism, leisure and boredom. The society of tomorrow must not be accessible only to an elite who control wealth, resources and technology, but on the contrary must be a social elevator for everyone, that meets their priorities. Friendship, lasting happiness and transcendent faith are life ideals lofty enough to nurture social connection and the hope each person needs.

A new humanism is in motion. The extraordinary progress we have made in the last one hundred and fifty years has generated personal and group momentum for humanity and created conditions for continuous growth of the world's population. We have pushed back the boundaries of individual needs and comforts, increasing wealth but also inequality.

Different political systems have been put to the test these past hundred years: monarchies, democracies, totalitarianism, republics, socialism and capitalism. Some have disappeared, others are still in place. The political challenges of the new century rest upon the issues of globalization and patriotism. Both pursue paths which are different but occasionally parallel or even convergent in places. In democracies, the people elect temporary governments, from a multipolar spectrum. The tensions between the two superpowers, America and China, have international repercussions and are pushing the Europe of member states towards developing geopolitical alliances. The fundamental values of the republic born of freedom of conscience are being damaged by religious fundamentalism, and the freedom of conscience that is one of the pillars of the 1948 Universal Declaration of Human Rights, "the advent of a world in which human beings shall enjoy freedom of speech and belief and freedom from

Tradition is the bulwark against standardization and the mediocrity of feelings and ideas.

fear and want," is being sorely tested. The freedom to believe and religious pluralism are non-negotiable premises just as every school of thought must respect the art of living together in peace and harmony. "Universalism must not be incompatible with patriotism." (Racine).

On an economic level, the appearance of hegemonic groups, primarily around new technologies, is disrupting the influence of the existing systems around petrochemical and international finance conglomerates. Governments are increasingly bound by and dependent on these dominant and often financially independent organizations.

We are witnessing an upsurge of tension and profoundly different visions with regard to the model to adopt. We must not confuse the globalization of the economy, and therefore trade, which is a sometimes aggressive and poorly regulated reality, with the globalization desired by some, which would be a regression from an anthropological point of view. The legitimacy of people begins with the deliberate fostering of individual sovereignty and the freedom to undertake, create and prosper while respecting others and the planet. The broadening of consciousness, transcendence, the freedom of feelings and respect for nature all support the advent of a new humanism, which will respect the universality of values without pitting communities against each other.

I am not naïve, nor insensitive to the difficulties stemming from the complexity of current problems, which have not found answers leading to lasting stability. The subtle balance that must be achieved rests upon a fundamental respect for the rights of each person and an innovative vision that breaks with the current models of domination.

I am a French patriot and a citizen of the world. I deeply love my country, its strength, its culture, its history, its tolerance, its geographical diversity as well as its complex character. To love one's country, respect its traditions and understand its identity are authentic acts, necessary for creating ties and learning to live together peacefully and supportive of each other. My wanderings on all continents for the past thirty years have enriched me and allowed me to understand better the aspirations and very different lifestyles of America, China, the African continent, Russia or Latin America. Everywhere I have felt the human soul, the desire to live, to exist and to create. Different cultures are a strength, roots which must be cherished and respected. Tradition is the bulwark against standardization and the mediocrity of feelings and ideas.

In the Internet age, we are all interconnected by the free flow of information. This vast deposit of learning, knowledge and both good and bogus news, demands of us the dependable ability to use discernment and a strong assertion of free will so as not to allow ourselves to be boxed in by a single, numbing current of thought. This discernment is needed to fight against all forms of outrageous oversimplification and stigmatization arising from attachment to religious coteries or schools of thought. Individual and collective emancipation happens through critical thinking, attentive listening and respect for difference.

Overuse of social networks has profoundly modified the behavior and minds of human beings, by redefining our connection to others and life in society, perceived through the lens of illusion and imagination, which are often rooted in a false reality. The loss of faith in the common, foundational values of a proven, community way of living creates the conditions for isolation.

It is time for the major democracies to redefine a bold social contract, one which will carry hope and collective harmony which avoid contraction and retreat upon ourselves, and encourage unobstructed communication between communities, whatever their origins and their ideas. This will only be possible by making individuals responsible, as opposed to dumbing down the public and controlling behaviors as is all too commonly practiced. The restriction of freedoms linked to Covid-19 containment measures says much about the fears and inadequacies apparent in many countries. The initial open-mindedness generated by the liberalization of trade, people and ideas is surreptitiously giving way to fencing people in and controlling them. This challenges emancipation and liberty, attributes which will need to be encouraged and protected.

Everywhere in the world I have discovered impassioned people, and a wealth of different codes of behavior, spectacular terrain, historical sites, natural parks and breathtaking landscapes. The splendor of the planet is like a garden of Eden, beautified by balanced ecosystems that harness living forces, connected to the energy of the unified cosmic field. This divine nature is at the service of humans but also of every living being. Its extraordinary organizational structure outlines perspectives for a new and more harmonious paradigm, in which development will not be the preserve of the few, but available to all. To prosper is not just to earn money or have power; rather it is mainly to give meaning to one's life and exist more intensely.

A close look at today's world, using the remarkable means of the 21st century, offers us a fascinating journey and opens the door to dazzling innovations which will revolutionize our way of life, and, should we so wish, the human community.

The current economies of the earth are founded upon energy, money, power and systems of domination and performance which increasingly centralize decisions while amplifying inequalities and anxieties. Continuous growth, paradoxically, has strengthened fears and unease.

In the 4th century BCE, Aristotle's role model Empedocles put forward the theory that the universe is made up of four elements: earth, water, air and fire. Contemporary to this, in China, the concept emerged of a cosmology in five phases, which are wood, fire, earth, metal and water, connected to yin and yang and to qi. This pattern connects the energies of the cosmos, nature, the seasons and living beings. Such a holistic vision establishes the link between microcosm and macrocosm, and defines the search for equilibrium required for the harmony of nature and the physical and mental health of human beings. In India, in the same period, the teachings of the Buddha emerged, with their four noble truths: *dukkha, samudaya, nirodha* and *magga*. The goal aspired to is the cessation of human suffering via an ascetic practice based on a path waymarked by guidelines for right living, an ideal of renunciation and the quest for nirvana. Humanity, the mastery of emotions, detachment, feelings, humility and inner peace are the principles extolled by the Buddha. In the Middle East, a succession of the descendants of Abraham established themselves between Jerusalem and Babylon, prophesying and strengthening a Judeo-Christian foundation. These various civilizations formed a common baseplate that rested upon principles, an ideal, a desire for harmony, a connection to the cosmos and transcendence. Living conditions were undeniably basic, learning was the preserve of a minority, and knowledge still very limited and mostly empirical, but spirituality thrived.

Every period is profitable and puts human organization to the test. All is temporary and transient; nature alone is eternal. We have come to the end of present-day systems which were developed by a materialism taken increasingly to extremes which has disrupted the forces of nature. It is time to raise our level of consciousness. Our starting point is the power of our volition and the liberation of our spiritual essence to attain harmony and offer a more fulfilling life for all, respect for difference and a new, far more protective and resilient relationship with the natural environment.

The growing need for energy on our planet is a serious challenge for humanity, now aware of the current breakdowns and the limits reached by our population of eight billion human beings in the areas of climate disruption, pollution and ever-greater quantities of waste. Decarbonization of the economy is an element in long-term agendas whose promises are binding only on those who believe in them. It is important to anticipate the post-oil era and find a new, innovative energy model. Atomic fission has produced energy which is clean from a carbon-emissions standpoint, but high-risk from an environmental one. Nevertheless, it has opened up a new avenue which has helped our societies to develop over the last fifty years. The world will need to find an energy source which is clean, carbon-free and unlimited, enabling us to get rid of pollution and restore the equilibria put under strain by global warming. Hydrogen is the most abundant element in the universe. Research efforts should concentrate on ways to utilize it at much reduced cost. Apart from that, energy generated by the wind, the sun and the cosmos itself represents an unlimited resource which we will be able to exploit if human ingenuity is directed towards ways of applying new discoveries.

The agriculture of the future will also display more respect for the environment, soils and subsoils. This will only be possible with the aid of governments that favor a health policy which, instead of being linked to medical care, is based on a redefinition of the benefits of a balanced diet based on local production and seasonality. Full awareness on the part of everyone and the spread of sources of supply meeting the criteria of sustainable production rules, without herbicides, will propel the process of transition to the restoration of natural systems and provide equal advantages for all.

In his Utopia, published in the 16th century, Thomas More writes: "Nature enjoins all men to help each other naturally and to share together in the joyful feast of life. This precept is just and reasonable; there is no individual raised so far above the human race that Providence need watch over him alone. Nature has given the same form to all: she comforts them with the same warmth, she embraces them all with the same love; that which she condemns is that one should increase his own well-being while compounding the misfortune of another." These precepts for living, in tune with nature, remain central to our concerns. This approach, which is bound up with the equilibrium of the ecosystems, will be attained through an open, creative and pluralist mode of organization, in harmony with the planet.

When economic, geopolitical, ecological and philosophical problems are all blended, the whole world is plunged into profound disarray which must at all costs be corrected. It is essential to analyze, understand and feel the hidden meaning of things, especially in the current period of upheaval. Nothing happens by chance. The problems being encountered by the human race with the Covid-19 pandemic bring to light the fragility of our system, the problems of coordination between states and our lack of foresight. It is difficult to fight against an invisible and insidious enemy which spreads very quickly and affects people very differently depending on their age, gender and state of health.

The media amplifier has increased people's fear, exaggerating the gravity of the situation. The unprecedented media circus has been blown up quite irrationally and has completely blocked out all other priorities. The world has been put under lockdown, and artificial respiration was applied not only to patients in a critical condition but also, more broadly and symbolically, by turns, to several billion people. It is important for health reasons to understand why and in what circumstances this epidemic began. Recent previous crises, such as SARS, the H1N1 virus or Ebola were always contained and did not impact every country.

People are traveling more around the world and information processing systems have developed considerably over the last ten years. We are all connected and the planet has become a garden. The Earth continues to orbit the sun, but our world has spun out of balance. We are confronted with an existential crisis. Are we going to draw the right conclusions and attempt to organize a new system, fairer, more equitable and offering hope to all?

In the last seventy years, we have created better living conditions, significantly reduced poverty, accumulated wealth and given access to education, health services, ample food, drinking water and civil rights to the majority of people. Regrettably, more than a billion people still live below the poverty threshold, but their number is diminishing. In the same period, in a manner completely unprecedented in all human history, we have degraded the soil, the oceans and the watercourses and created the conditions for a climatic collapse. Population growth has rocketed and many countries, especially in Africa, face an emergency. Biodiversity is under threat. The balance sheet is heavily negative, and many species of animals and plants have disappeared or are close to extinction.

The alarm sounded by militants, politicians and NGOs has not engendered a profound change in our social model. The COP global summits have not reached significant agreements, even if they have brought a gleam of hope with specific commitments to limit global warming.

We have to remain clear-headed and try to draw conclusions, keeping in mind the priorities of everyone, but also the subtle, delicate equilibrium of nature.

The COP global summits have not reached significant agreements, even if they have brought a gleam of hope with specific commitments to limit global warming.

The positive feature of the severely reduced international trade in 2020 is the drop in pollution and the improvement in air quality, especially in big cities. Lockdown has also enabled people to refocus their priorities on their families and friends and rediscover the simple pleasures of everyday life. On a more individual level, and in particular for the overworked, this period of quiet has provided an opportunity to take an inner breather and experience a different relationship with time. In contrast, the decision makers and chief executives have lived with the anxiety of falling sales and have had to second-guess the resumption of business, at a loss for points of reference.

The fight against this virus has had a transitory effect on the world economy and the way it is organized. The financial world, especially the Fed in the United States and, to a lesser degree, the ECB in Europe, has made every effort to prime the pump again, reassure investors and create the conditions for a recovery. On every continent, this process has been made easier by an increase of awareness and the needs that it gives rise to.

Some habits have changed. Teleworking has revealed its advantages and its efficiency. Videoconferencing, which is becoming widespread, can greatly reduce the carbon footprint and the number of travelers. A new economy, less polluting, more hedonistic and directed towards new needs, will create opportunities and generate new jobs, especially in the fields of health, farming and leisure. The civilization of the automobile is past: metropolitan centers now offer new modes of local travel. Car sharing, rail, public transport, electric vehicles and cycling are developing and could become prevalent.

Respect for soils and subsoils through organic farming, biodynamics or permaculture creates awareness and brings back the real taste of food, while improving its keeping properties. The advice of nutritionists, dieticians and medical practitioners fosters bodily harmony and facilitates a more holistic approach. The circular economy and the renewal of local production must be encouraged, as they save energy, water and raw materials.

This sustainable model helps us understand the extent to which the resources of the planet are limited. It is in direct opposition to the linear model, in which products are developed, manufactured, consumed and thrown away. This consumerist archetype has revealed its limits and creates too much waste, including the pollution generated by plant protection products, the disposal of plastics, 10 percent of which end up in the oceans and, more subtly, the creation of artificial needs, such as the consumption of out-of-season fruits. Fortunately, young people are seeking to feed themselves better and are rediscovering a taste for cooking and healthy, better balanced meals.

The distinctiveness of human beings is symbolized by their emotional capacity and their determination to adapt. This opening of hearts generates hope in difficult circumstances. When we stop thinking and analyzing and just let ourselves be guided by our inner being, the best often becomes possible.

More profoundly, the fresh look being taken by the young opens the door to a different life plan, taking account of the seasons and renewing the connection with nature. This is fertile ground, promising change favorable to the coming generations and bringing harmony between town and country. A new model of extensive farming, more resilient and sustainable, could induce the mass retailers to strengthen multi-year partnerships with producers. Other forms of retailing around residential areas, such as local markets, specialty stores and organic grocers, not to mention daily vegetable boxes sold online, constitute convenient new supply models offering quality.

We need to seize the opportunity and use the advantages offered by this remarkable moment in the history of the world so that every financial partner offers conditions of access to bank credits no longer based solely on short-term profit but favorable to constructive, sustainable projects beneficial to the equilibrium of the planet. Crowdfunding platforms already exist: they could be available for projects on diverse scales so that opportunities are available for all.

The adventure of agriculture is an element offering income in the long term. It is subject to the vagaries of chance, but guarantees a return on investment over time. The capital invested grows with time, because the value of the production tool grows inexorably. Differentiation, innovation and creativity bring far from negligible capital gains. This will come through the award of quality labels, precision agriculture, a striving for naturalness and the diversity of products, seeds and varieties. Polyculture also combats the impoverishment of soils, creates more harmonious environments and enables better pollination, which is vital to our survival.

Every vital truth seems utopian initially. "The problems of the world cannot possibly be solved by skeptics or cynics whose horizons are limited by the obvious realities. We need men who can dream of things that never were," wrote John Fitzgerald Kennedy.

The road maps set out by some governments for the ecological transition require improvement in several areas: first of all, states must realize that, if the concept is to be successful, it is time to position it among our individual and collective priorities on the planetary scale, in a joint endeavor of solidarity and generosity. The heightened awareness of 2020 creates the conditions for this shared vision and common itinerary based on clearly identified principles. Meaningful change will be impossible without a common goal shared by the twenty largest countries. Each of them must participate towards this existential cause, because it is beautiful, noble and useful, and will bring into being a better, more protective world.

This new paradigm is desired by all who wish to live in harmony with nature while providing for the essential needs of every individual. Governments have a duty to go beyond specific interests and the mechanisms of domination and power.

The economy must also be reinvented, leaving room for social and environmental adaptation based on research, innovation and the expansion of a carbon-neutral society, but also on cooperation and fairer distribution of the value added between sectors. An economic concept more oriented towards solidarity will enable renewed local production on a massive scale of the products needed for life in society and will avoid, on principle, the destructive overbidding that goes with productivity-oriented models, which scorn the life of the soil and respect for people.

The European continent is at the crossroads of its destiny. The idea of Europe as a unified entity came into being in 1957, but now new life equal to the challenge of a single market of five hundred million people must be breathed into it. It could become an exemplar of resilience and the creation of wealth and progress for humanity. The green economy and respect for biodiversity are cross-border concepts needing the support of European financing. Europe's investment capacity is intact, while its countries are too indebted to meet this requirement.

Every vital truth seems utopian initially. "The problems of the world cannot possibly be solved by skeptics or cynics whose horizons are limited by the obvious realities. We need men who can dream of things that never were," wrote John Fitzgerald Kennedy. It is now vital to be present at the start of this new era to bring out the best in everyone and guarantee sustainable growth and a better life. Geopolitics, narrow party interests and the mechanisms of domination are now merely the tools of another age. The world needs to respect the deep-seated aspirations of people and their cultures, but also to achieve global interconnection and long-term agreements centered on strong principles, as well as a joint road map as powerful and all-embracing as the Universal Declaration of Human Rights of 10 December 1948. In the coming months, a new charter must be written embodying ethics, solidarity, resilience, sustainability and empathy, and rewarding for the human race.

Humankind is in a dominant position with regard to nature and the living world. It is urgent and indispensable that we realize the problems involved in respecting all fauna and flora in a living environment that displays more respect and sympathy for the weaker members. The same applies to forests, seas and landscapes. The subtle balances of nature, oxygen production and carbon capture by trees, the production of plankton in the oceans – an essential element in the food chain – or temperature control by the forest canopy are all endangered ecosystems.

If the existing leaders and systems fail at this historic moment, they will be responsible for the resulting chaos, the return to isolation and the end of Europe and multilateral agreements. They will make way for another type of organization dominated by corporations forming a hegemony without frontiers, with the potential for creating digital dictatorships, dehumanized and with the sole objective of profit for a tiny minority.

The fundamental equilibria and the guiding principles must be guaranteed in their turn by states, international institutions and the general public, with a duty of transparency, an ideal of liberty and fraternity, revived biodiversity and better living conditions excluding all discrimination with regard to color, gender, origin or creed, but with open hearts, beating in synchrony.

Let us all unite to be equal to the task ahead.

BE THE CHANGE.

APPENDICES

BIBLIOGRAPHY

Rudolf Steiner, *Le Cours aux agriculteurs,* éditions Novalis, Montesson, 2003 (third edition).

Stéphane Cardinaux, *Géométries sacrées,* éditions Trajectoire, Escalquens, 2004.

Nicolas Joly, *Le Vin, du ciel à la terre : la viticulture en biodynamie,* éditions Libre et Solidaire, Paris, 2019.

Prof. Vincent Castronovo, University of Liège, *Le Microbiote intestinal au service de notre santé,* lecture, 29 septembre 2017, Youtube.

The Bible, Old and New Testaments.

TABLE OF CONTENTS

Editorial management: Nicolas de Cointet, Éditions Albin Michel
Translation: Mark and James Harvey
Cover: Franklin Labbé
Layout: Alexandrea Roucheray
Portrait on the band: Photo © Ulrich Lebeuf

Printed in France (CPI Bussière - 2062192)
for ACC Art Books Ltd., Woodbridge, Suffolk, UK

www.accartbooks.com

ACC
ART
BOOKS

PEFC™
10-31-3068

PEFC Certified

This product is from
sustainably managed
forests and controlled
sources

www.pefc.co.uk